CQ's Supreme Court Simulation

CQ's Supreme Court Simulation

Government in Action

Julie Dolan
Macalester College

and

Marni Ezra
Hood College

CQ PRESS

A Division of Congressional Quarterly Inc.
Washington, D.C.

CQ Press
1255 22nd Street, N.W., Suite 400
Washington, D.C. 20037

202-822-1475; 800-638-1710

www.cqpress.com

Cover and interior designs: Karen Doody

Printed and bound in the United States of America

05   04   03   02   01   5   4   3   2   1

Library of Congress Cataloging-in-Publication Data
In process
  ISBN 1-56802-710-9

To Our Parents

Contents

Foreword

CQ Press is pleased to introduce a new line of educational tools designed to incorporate traditionally researched topics into a learning environment. The long-awaited Government in Action series offers firsthand experience on the workings of the government. Whether read in the library by patrons interested in learning about the government or used in the classroom by students and instructors, the Government in Action series is a rich classroom-tested tool that will benefit anyone seeking to gain a better understanding of how our democracy works. Volumes in the series include *CQ's Legislative Simulation: Government in Action*, *CQ's White House Media Simulation: Government in Action*, *CQ's Congressional Election Simulation: Government in Action*, and *CQ's Supreme Court Simulation: Government in Action*.

To enhance the simulation experience, a free instructor's manual on how to conduct a classroom simulation is offered on the Web at http://library.cqpress.com/gia. Whether you are encouraging library research or conducting classroom simulations, the Government in Action series is an ideal reference tool. We are very interested in your impression of our new series, and we encourage you to send your feedback to GIAFeedback@cqpress.com.

CQ Press

Preface

Although the Framers of the Constitution considered the Supreme Court to be, as Alexander Hamilton put it in the *Federalist Papers*, "beyond comparison the weakest of the three departments of power," the decisions the Court renders have a great impact on American citizens' lives. From school segregation, to a woman's right to choose abortion, to an arrestee's right to counsel, the Supreme Court's effect on public policy in the United States cannot be ignored. Indeed, the Court makes decisions each year that profoundly affect the relationship between American citizens and their government. Nevertheless, the Court remains the least understood of the three branches of government. Many students of American government have never taken a judicial politics course or can even name the chief justice of the United States.

This book attempts to provide readers with an up-close and personal look at the workings of the U.S. Supreme Court. By taking on the role of a Supreme Court justice, a lawyer arguing a case before the Court, or an interest group official trying to sway the Court through written briefs, each participant in this simulation will become familiar with the processes the Court follows in carrying out its responsibilities. In addition, the difficulties encountered by the justices when deciding difficult cases and controversies will become more apparent.

Part I of the book consists of two chapters. The first explains the workings and procedures of the Supreme Court, walking the reader through the various stages of a case that is sent to the Court for review. It discusses how a case reaches the Supreme Court, how the Court decides whether to accept it, how lawyers on both sides of the controversy use formal oral argument to persuade the justices that their arguments are compelling and worthy, how the justices meet to discuss the cases they have

heard, and how they eventually write the opinions that capture and explain the Court's legal reasoning.

Chapter 2 is a guide to the roles and responsibilities of the players in the simulation. There are a variety of possible roles to play, including those of the chief justice and eight associate justices, the lawyers for both sides of the controversy, the clerk of the Court, and representatives of interest groups and others who participate as "friends of the court."

Part II includes copies of the cases to be simulated, along with supplementary background readings on the issues presented in the cases.

Acknowledgments

We wish to thank a number of people for their helpful comments and support in getting this book published. First we thank Adrian Forman of CQ Press for overseeing this project from beginning to end, along with Shana Wagger and Carolyn Goldinger for their remarkable attention to detail throughout the editing process and Sally Ryman for her skillful handling of production. We also thank our colleagues, Joseph L. Daly, Harry N. Hirsch, Karen O'Connor, Barbara Palmer, Cameron Parkhurst, and David H. Rosenbloom, all of whom offered numerous helpful suggestions. In addition, we thank our student assistants Julie Fouché and Megan Mills, who spent hours reading drafts, conducting background research, and hunting down additional material. We could not have completed this book without such great support and assistance.

Julie Dolan
Marni Ezra

PART I

A Supreme Court Primer

CHAPTER 1

Supreme Court Procedures and Players

"It is the most mysterious, remote, and least understood branch of American government."

WETA-TV, This Honorable Court

As the quotation above attests, the judiciary is the most enigmatic branch of the United States government. In stark contrast to round-the-clock televised C-SPAN coverage of the U.S. House of Representatives and U.S. Senate, the Supreme Court of the United States forbids all video and still cameras in its courtroom and chambers. The nine members—the chief justice and eight associate justices—conduct most of their decision making in confidential meetings at which neither staff nor any member of the public is allowed, adding further mystery to the work of the highest court in the land. The fact that only 8 percent of the American public can correctly identify the chief justice of the United States and that only 17 percent can name even three justices demonstrates the lack of basic public knowledge about the U.S. Supreme Court.[1] (See

box "Members of the U.S. Supreme Court and Dates of Appointment.")

The work of the Court continues all year, but the justices generally sit in session only from October through May. They continue to hand down decisions through late June or early July. While in session, the justices hear oral arguments on cases that have been granted hearings, decide which cases to hear during the next term, hold conferences to discuss the ongoing proceedings of the Court, and write and release legal opinions on the cases they have decided. Unlike members of the executive and legislative branches, whose ideas and opinions are instantly available through the media, the members of the Court are rarely visible to the American public. They appear in Court only to hear oral arguments or for the rare reading of an opinion from the bench. In writing their opinions, members of the Court are assisted by their clerks, but the public is not privy to their thoughts until the final opinions are released.

This chapter describes the processes and procedures the Court uses to carry out its responsibilities as the court of last resort and leader of the judicial branch of the United States. After a brief look at the Framers' intentions for the judiciary, the chapter explains how cases arrive at the Court, why the justices consider only a small fraction of the petitions they receive, how lawyers on both sides of a case use oral argument to attempt to persuade the justices to rule in their favor, and how the justices make their decisions.

Constitutional Powers Granted to the Supreme Court

Comparing the judicial branch of government with the legislative and executive branches provides some clues about the Framers' thinking about the role of the judici-

---

MEMBERS OF THE U.S. SUPREME COURT AND DATES OF APPOINTMENT

1. Chief Justice William H. Rehnquist (chief justice 1986– ; associate justice 1971–1986)
2. Associate Justice John Paul Stevens (1975–)
3. Associate Justice Sandra Day O'Connor (1981–)
4. Associate Justice Antonin Scalia (1986–)
5. Associate Justice Anthony M. Kennedy (1988–)
6. Associate Justice David H. Souter (1990–)
7. Associate Justice Clarence Thomas (1991–)
8. Associate Justice Ruth Bader Ginsburg (1993–)
9. Associate Justice Stephen G. Breyer (1994–)

ary in American governance. The Framers believed that the legislature would necessarily predominate in the new government, and one glance at the number and depth of legislative powers outlined in the U.S. Constitution makes their intentions clear. Article I, which spells out the wide variety of powers to be exercised by the legislature, contains ten lengthy and relatively detailed sections. Moreover, the placement of the legislature's powers first in the Constitution is a clear indication of the importance the Framers accorded to the legislature. The powers and responsibilities of the president appear next in the Constitution, encapsulated in four relatively short sections. The powers of the judiciary do not appear until Article III, which consists of only three very short sections. All in all, about 3,000 words are devoted to describing the shape, form, and powers of Congress and the presidency, while a mere 400 describe the nature and powers of the judiciary.

The amount of attention devoted to the three branches of government within the Federalist Papers provides further evidence. The Federalist Papers are a series of essays published in New York newspapers from 1787 to 1788, explaining how the new government would operate and arguing for the ratification of the new U.S. Constitution. These essays are widely regarded as an excellent source of the Framers' thoughts and intentions in creating the new government. Of the eighty-five Federalist Papers, at least fifteen are devoted to Congress, while only six address the judicial branch.

As might be expected, the Constitution is not specific about the powers of the Supreme Court. Article III simply refers to "the judicial power" without clearly identifying what this power will be. In Federalist Paper No. 78, Alexander Hamilton states that the power of the judiciary is to exercise judgment and to make sure that the principles of the Constitution are upheld, but he also argues that "the judiciary is beyond comparison the weakest of the three departments of power." Nevertheless, the judiciary was expected to serve an important role in the new nation. As Hamilton explains, "[A] constitution is, in fact, and must be regarded by the judges, as a fundamental law. It therefore belongs to them to ascertain its meaning, as well as the meaning of any particular act proceeding from the legislative body."[2] In carrying out these responsibilities, the Supreme Court has overturned more than 100 acts of Congress and more than 1,000 acts enacted by state and local governments,[3] making it quite an influential player in American government after all. Even though the Framers did not clearly delineate specific powers to be exercised by the Supreme Court, its power to affect public policy should not be underestimated.

What Types of Cases Is the Supreme Court Authorized to Hear? Original and Appellate Jurisdiction

The Constitution says that judicial power "shall be vested in one supreme Court, and in such inferior Courts as the Congress may from time to time ordain and establish" and that the Supreme Court will exercise both original jurisdiction and appellate jurisdiction (Art. III, Sect. 1 and 2). Original jurisdiction means that the Supreme Court will be the first and only court of law to adjudicate particular kinds of the controversies. An example is a case in which two states are parties to a dispute. In *Kansas v. Colorado*, which was argued before the Court during its 2000–2001 term, the dispute between the two states was over the use of the Arkansas River.[4] The vast majority of cases that come before the Supreme Court, however, do so under its appellate jurisdiction, which is its right to hear cases that have been appealed from elsewhere in the judicial system.[5] The Court is not required to hear all of the cases that are appealed from lower courts; rather, it has a great deal of latitude to decide which of the thousands of cases submitted will ultimately be heard. The next section explains the source and nature of this power in further detail.

Discretionary Jurisdiction

Unlike many other courts of law, the Supreme Court is not required to accept all requests for a hearing. Instead, the Court has discretionary jurisdiction. The Constitution makes no mention of discretionary jurisdiction, and it took an act of Congress to grant the Court such power. The Judiciary Act of 1925 says that the Supreme Court may elect to hear or deny most cases based on their merits.[6] With nearly 9,000 cases filed each year, the Supreme Court picks and chooses a fraction—about 100 per year—to hear.[7] This distinction separates the Supreme Court from the other courts in the United States. Most appeals courts are obliged to hear all cases that are brought before them, but the Supreme Court has the luxury of hearing only those cases that the justices believe are sufficiently "ripe" and meritorious. In the 2000–2001 term, the Court heard only eighty-six cases.[8] Discretionary jurisdiction thus enables the members of the Supreme Court to pay sustained attention to those cases they deem most pressing and significant.

How Cases Arrive at the Supreme Court

Generally speaking, the Supreme Court will hear cases on appeal only if the parties to the case have first exhausted all other judicial avenues. Cases originating in both the federal and states' court systems may petition the Supreme Court for a hearing but generally must first proceed through the lower courts. In the federal court system, most cases begin in one of the ninety-four federal district courts. If, for example, a litigant is not satisfied with a district court ruling, he or she may submit an appeal to have the case heard by one of the twelve federal appeals courts. After the appeals court issues a decision, an unsatisfied litigant would then be able to appeal to the U.S. Supreme Court.

There are, however, some exceptions. Slightly different rules of procedure govern criminal and civil court cases. In criminal cases, or those cases dealing with matters contained within U.S. or state penal statutes, prosecutors (the government's attorneys) and defendants do not have the same rights to appeal cases to a higher court. The prosecuting attorney cannot appeal a "not guilty" verdict be-

cause doing so would constitute double jeopardy (trying a defendant twice for the same crime), which is forbidden by the Fifth Amendment to the U.S. Constitution. In civil cases, which generally deal with disputes between private parties and involve no criminal behavior, both parties to the dispute have the right to appeal a court's decision at both the district and appellate court level.

In the states' court systems, most cases go through a similar process, beginning with a district court, proceeding to an appeals court, and finally ending up at the state supreme court. After reaching the highest court in the state system, such as the state supreme court, a litigant may then appeal his or her case to the Supreme Court, provided it deals with a substantial federal question such as a perceived violation of constitutional rights.[9] (See box "How a Case Gets to the United States Supreme Court.") Otherwise, the Supreme Court will refuse to hear the case.

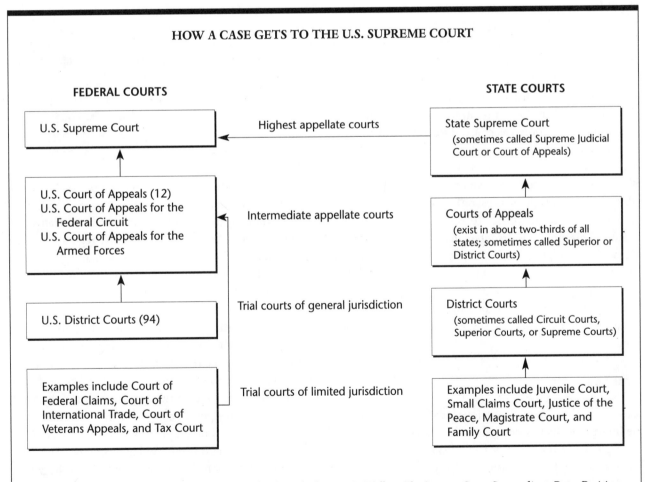

HOW A CASE GETS TO THE U.S. SUPREME COURT

FEDERAL COURTS | | **STATE COURTS**

Federal Courts		State Courts
U.S. Supreme Court	Highest appellate courts	State Supreme Court (sometimes called Supreme Judicial Court or Court of Appeals)
U.S. Court of Appeals (12) U.S. Court of Appeals for the Federal Circuit U.S. Court of Appeals for the Armed Forces	Intermediate appellate courts	Courts of Appeals (exist in about two-thirds of all states; sometimes called Superior or District Courts)
U.S. District Courts (94)	Trial courts of general jurisdiction	District Courts (sometimes called Circuit Courts, Superior Courts, or Supreme Courts)
Examples include Court of Federal Claims, Court of International Trade, Court of Veterans Appeals, and Tax Court	Trial courts of limited jurisdiction	Examples include Juvenile Court, Small Claims Court, Justice of the Peace, Magistrate Court, and Family Court

Source: Lee Epstein, Jeffrey A. Segal, Harold J. Spaeth, and Thomas G. Walker, *The Supreme Court Compendium: Data, Decisions, and Developments*, 2d ed. (Washington, D.C.: CQ Press, 1996), 650.

Judicial Review and Legal Reasoning

The Supreme Court exercises what is referred to as judicial review, which is the right to review and declare unconstitutional acts of other branches of government. This power is not spelled out in the Constitution. Most people today take for granted the Court's role in determining the constitutionality of laws and government regulations, but it took a dispute over a minor provision of the Judiciary Act of 1789 before the Court assumed such power. In the landmark case of *Marbury v. Madison* (1803), the Supreme Court for the first time invalidated a provision of law passed by Congress. At issue was a section of the Judiciary Act that gave the U.S. Supreme Court the authority to issue writs of mandamus, orders instructing government officials to perform particular duties. In *Marbury v. Madison* the Court concluded that Congress had erred in granting it the power to issue such writs, as the legislature was, in effect, expanding the jurisdiction of the Supreme Court beyond that specified in the U.S. Constitution.[10] Because the authority of the Constitution supersedes that of laws passed by the legislature, as Chief Justice John Marshall explained in the opinion of the Court, the power granted by Congress to issue writs of mandamus was unconstitutional. Marshall further clarified the power of the judiciary, declaring, "It is, emphatically, the province and duty of the judicial department, to say what the law is." Since then, the Court has enjoyed the power of judicial review.[11]

How do the members of the Court use the power of judicial review? The Court is not free to reach out and identify unconstitutional laws; rather, it must wait for parties with real controversies to bring their cases to the Court. (This process is described in the section "The Certiorari Process.") Further, the Supreme Court is not a trial court, and so does not deal with witnesses, juries, or evidence. How, then, do the justices make decisions? The next section describes three tools the Court relies upon for decision making: prior case law, precedent, and statutory language.

Case Law

Case law is the sum of all previous judicial rulings and can be interpreted as law created by the judicial branch. For example, when the Supreme Court established a trimester system for regulating abortions in the United States in the landmark *Roe v. Wade* case, it effectively dictated to the state legislatures what they could and could not do in regard to restricting women's access to abortion. According to the decision, the states could not interfere with a woman's choice to obtain an abortion in the first three months of her pregnancy. This ruling was binding on the states and other courts, giving it the weight of law.

Precedent

Case law creates precedent, the legal principle that past decisions, unless overturned, form the basis for future decisions. For example, in deciding *Roe v. Wade*, the justices drew on a precedent set eight years earlier in *Griswold v. Connecticut*, in which the Court's opinion established a basic right to privacy. The justices extended this line of reasoning in *Roe v. Wade* to declare that a woman's right to privacy included unfettered access to abortion in the first trimester of pregnancy. The practice of honoring and upholding precedent is known as *stare decisis*, literally "let the decision stand." Previous decisions are overturned from time to time, but not lightheartedly. A more dramatic example of the Court's reliance on precedent was its adherence to the *Plessy v. Ferguson* ruling declaring that racially segregated railroad cars were separate but equal and thus not in violation of the Equal Protection Clause of the Fourteenth Amendment. The Court upheld this ruling for more than fifty years until the *Brown v. Board of Education* opinion struck down separate public schools for blacks and whites, ruling that separate could never be equal.

Statutory Intent

The final decision-making tool is statutory or legislative intent, which the Supreme Court examines when interpreting the constitutionality of a law or administrative regulation. Because laws and administrative regulations must accommodate the diverse interests of many groups and individuals, they are often broadly written and may lack the particular details necessary for members of the public and courts to understand their meanings and intentions. In these cases, the Court may examine the public record and history of the law or regulation in question in an attempt to discern the real intention and goal of the statute so as to rule upon its constitutionality. For example, *Russell/Stearns v. Gregoire* (1997), a case heard by the Ninth Circuit Court of Appeals, concerned the constitutionality of a state law authorizing community notification programs. In Washington State, Willie Russell was convicted for a sex offense and served his time. While he was in prison, the state passed a law requiring that all incarcerated sex offenders notify local law enforcement authorities as to their whereabouts when released. For certain levels of sex offenses, information about the approximate area where the offender lives can be released to the public. Russell sued, claiming that the state was violating his rights to privacy and due process and that he was being further punished by the community notification provisions, which effectively branded him as a dangerous criminal after he had served his time. In examining his claim, the U.S. Court of Appeals for the Ninth Circuit went back to the statute to see whether its intention was to inflict further punishment on sex offenders or to serve some other important governmental purpose. The appeals court ruled against Russell, arguing that the law had no punitive intent but was crafted for the benefit of the community so that citizens could protect themselves from potentially dangerous sex offenders. Thus, because punishment was not intended by the statute, Russell's claim was denied. He eventually appealed his case to the U.S. Supreme Court, but the justices declined to accept it.

The Certiorari Process

How do the justices decide which cases to hear? The Supreme Court requires most of those seeking to appear before it to file petitions for writ of certiorari, legal briefs that summarize the litigants' reasoning and explain why they should be granted a hearing. In crafting a petition for certiorari, the petitioner (the person or group who is seeking legal redress through the Supreme Court) draws from precedent, the facts of the particular case, and other legal rulings to show how a lower court erred in deciding his or her case and why it is necessary for the Supreme Court to grant a writ of certiorari (an order by the Supreme Court to a lower court to send the case up for review).[12]

Although the vast majority of cases follow this route to the Court, there are a few additional ways by which cases arrive at the Court. As already mentioned, the Supreme Court has original jurisdiction over some cases. Petitioners in these cases do not file a petition for writ of certiorari, but submit a different type of brief asking the Court to hear their case. A few cases come to the Court on a writ of appeal. Most are deemed important enough by Congress to receive special attention and therefore arrive at the Supreme Court in an expedited fashion. After such a case is heard first by special three-judge district courts, any further appeals go directly to the Supreme Court.[13] Last, a small number of cases come to the Supreme Court through a writ of certification. The U.S. courts of appeals use this route to seek clarification from the Supreme Court on a matter of law not yet decided.[14]

Winnowing Down the List

The Court receives about 9,000 petitions for certiorari each year, or approximately 175 cases per week.[15] To wade through the extensive paperwork and decide which cases merit consideration, the justices rely heavily on their law clerks, recent law school graduates hired by the Court to assist the justices in carrying out their responsibilities. Most of the justices participate in what is known as the "cert pool," a group of the justices' law clerks. The pool divides up the labor at the certiorari stage by reading over and summarizing the hundreds of petitions received weekly and then reports back to the justices with pool memos. These memos summarize the facts of the case and the legal issues at hand and recommend whether the case should be granted cert.[16] By dividing up the cert petitions, the pool conserves time and resources.[17]

The Discuss List

The nine justices meet in conference on a weekly basis to discuss the cases on the cert lists, but before they gather the chief justice circulates what is known as the "discuss list," which contains those cases the chief justice believes are worthy of conference deliberation. The chief justice generates the discuss list, but other justices may add cases to it. A fairly small percentage of cases submitted to the Supreme Court ever make it this far in the process. Two judicial scholars estimate that only about 20 percent to 30 percent of the cases submitted appear on the discuss list, and Justice Ruth Bader Ginsburg estimates that the percentage is even lower, something like 10 percent to 13 percent.[18] Further, less than a third of these cases are granted cert.[19] The cases that do not make the discuss list are automatically denied certiorari.

Conference to Discuss Petitions for Certiorari

The chief justice presides over the certiorari conference, setting the agenda and beginning the discussion of the cases before the justices. The discussion proceeds by seniority: after the chief justice speaks about the first case, the next most senior justice speaks about it, also indicating whether the case should be granted or denied cert. This pattern continues until all of the justices have had a chance to speak, indicating whether they think the case should be heard. Four votes are necessary for a case to be granted a hearing, the so-called "Rule of Four." If four justices agree to hear a case, it will be granted a writ of certiorari and both sides of the dispute will be invited to present their oral arguments before the Court.[20] The cases that do not receive at least four votes are denied certiorari.

When the Court denies certiorari in a particular case, the media often declare that the Court has affirmed the lower court ruling. That assumption is not exactly correct. Instead, the decision to deny certiorari simply indicates that the Court will not hear this particular case at this particular time. The lower court ruling remains intact if the Court refuses to revisit the issue, but the justices are not necessarily signaling that they agree with the lower court ruling. The Court may refuse to hear the case because it is waiting for a better case to come along, one with a set of facts more suitable for ruling on the constitutional issues at stake. For example, in the 1990s litigants petitioned the Supreme Court to hear cases involving school vouchers and public university affirmative action programs, but the Court declined certiorari in both cases (*Jackson v. Benson*, denied cert in 1998; *Texas v. Hopwood*, denied cert in 1996). These denials do not indicate that the justices have made a decision about the constitutionality of the programs, but that they decided not to hear these particular cases. In denying cert to *Texas v. Hopwood*, Justice Ginsburg noted that the affirmative action program in question was no longer in effect and so the Court "must await a final judgment on a program genuinely in controversy before addressing the important question raised in this petition." That is not to say, however, that the Court will refuse to hear all future challenges to affirmative action programs in public universities.

Factors That Affect Justices' Decisions on Cert

What factors affect the justices' decisions to grant or deny cert? A variety of factors are often cited. The Court usually considers whether a case deals with a federal or constitutional issue, if the case is timely and of general applicability, and whether ruling on the case will resolve legal conflicts percolating through the court system. Cases that meet most or all of these criteria have a much better chance of being heard than cases that meet a few or only one. If a case does not deal with "a substantial federal question," the Court will not accept it. On the issues of general applicability and resolving legal conflicts, a quote from a former Supreme Court clerk is instructive. To new law clerks faced with summarizing stacks of petitions for certiorari, he explains,

> As you go through each one, you'll get a feel for whether the petition raises an issue that is a matter of some controversy or whether it's

very specific to that litigation. The buzzword around here is factbound—that means that the case is of great concern to the litigants but the Court's resolution of it won't help the other courts in dealing with their caseload.[21]

Thus, the Court prefers cases that are not so narrowly tailored to the litigants in the particular case so as to be of little use to the lower courts.

Controversy among lower courts also affects whether a case lands on the Court's docket, as articulated by Justice Sandra Day O'Connor:

> We take cases, generally speaking, because other courts around the country have reached conflicting results on that issue. And most of the cases we take are ones in which very good arguments can be made on each side of the question.[22]

Chief Justice William Rehnquist makes a similar point:

> There are really only two or three factors comprised in the certiorari decision—conflict with other courts, general importance, and perception that the decision is wrong in the light of Supreme Court precedent.[23]

Other scholars have shown that the presence of the U.S. government as a petitioner on a case increases the chances that the Court will grant cert, as does the presence of amicus curiae briefs.[24] Amicus curiae briefs are legal documents filed by parties who are not named in the suit but have a particular interest in the outcome. These briefs are submitted by interested "friends of the court" (the literal translation of amicus curiae) both during the certiorari stage and after the Court has accepted a case for review. Like the briefs submitted by the litigants to the dispute, amicus curiae briefs spell out the arguments that favor one side over the other. For example, when free speech suits are filed, the American Civil Liberties Union often submits amicus curiae briefs, defending the rights of the litigant to exercise his or her free speech rights.

Submitting Briefs

After a case has been granted certiorari, the clerk of the Court notifies the parties and asks them to prepare and submit written briefs to the Court. The petitioner is allowed forty-five days after the Court grants cert to submit a brief, while the respondent has an additional thirty days after receiving the petitioner's brief to file its brief with the Court.[25] This lead time allows the justices plenty of time to read and digest the briefs and to prepare questions prior to the lawyers' appearance before the Court.

Oral Argument

The Court hears oral argument on Mondays, Tuesdays, and Wednesdays from October through April, with a few exceptions. Oral argument begins at 10:00 a.m. and ends at 3:00 p.m., with an hour recess at noon for lunch. Each case takes an hour to hear. The marshal announces the arrival of the justices for the 10 a.m. case, and those present in the courtroom rise. After everyone is seated, the Court proceeds to take care of any preliminary matters.

What is the purpose of oral argument? Oral argument presents an opportunity for counsel on each side to put forth their strongest arguments on the case and to attempt to convince the justices of the correctness of their legal claims. The justices read the legal briefs submitted by counsel prior to arriving for oral argument and therefore do not need a rundown of the entire written brief and all of its arguments. The Court emphasizes that "[o]ral arguments are not designed to summarize briefs, but present the opportunity to stress the main issues of the case that might persuade the Court in your favor."[26]

On preparing for oral argument, Bruce Neuborne of New York University Law School emphasizes the value of doing one's homework before arriving at the Court:

> The role of a lawyer going up to the Supreme Court is to assemble a coalition of five votes.... All of us are acutely conscious of the voting patterns of the various Justices and what we do is we try to plug the case into those voting patterns to maximize the chance that five of them, based on the past voting patterns, will vote with us on this particular case.[27]

The chief justice presides over oral arguments, beginning with opening remarks and announcing the docket number of the case before the Court, then acknowledging the lawyers for both sides and inviting them to deliver their remarks, and finally, bringing the oral arguments to a close. The petitioner presents his or her argument first, after being acknowledged by the chief justice, who says "Mr./Ms. [insert name of Petitioner here], you may proceed whenever you're ready."[28] Counsel for the petitioner begins with "Mr. Chief Justice and may it please the Court..." and then starts his or her prepared remarks. Attorneys for each side are allowed thirty minutes to present their case. During this time, the attorneys are routinely peppered with questions from the bench.

The Supreme Court publishes a guide for attorneys appearing before it. In *Guide for Counsel* the clerk of the Court tells lawyers about Court protocol and what behavior to expect from the justices. Lawyers should not be surprised to be interrupted fairly early in their remarks. In fact, most attorneys do not get more than a few minutes into their prepared statements before the questioning begins. The guide advises counsel to eliminate about half of what they originally planned to cover during oral argument, reminding them that "your allotted time evaporates quickly, especially when numerous questions come from the Court."[29] To deal with such time constraints, lawyers are advised to skip most of their arguments and emphasize their strongest points.

The *Guide for Counsel* also provides advice for showing proper respect and decorum before the bench. First, the justices should never be referred to by their first names, but always by Justice So-and-So or Your Honor. The only exception is reserved for the chief justice, who is referred to as Mr. Chief Justice (or Ms. Chief Justice, if a female ever attains this position). Second, counsel should never interrupt a justice who is speaking and should cease speaking immediately whenever a justice interrupts. Finally, the *Guide* advises that counsel make every attempt possible to answer the questions posed by the justices. To these ends, lawyers should anticipate the likely questions from the justices and be prepared to answer them, be well-versed in the facts and legal matters at issue, and be thoroughly familiar with the business of their clients.

With five minutes remaining in counsel's time, the marshal, the official timekeeper, activates a white light, signaling that the attorney should begin wrapping up his or her arguments. After the five minutes have expired, a red light goes on, signaling that the lawyer should stop talking and sit down immediately, unless he or she is in the middle of answering a question from the bench. Under these circumstances, the attorney may finish answering the question and any others a justice asks.[30] After both sides have presented their argument and responded to questions, the chief justice announces that "the case is submitted."[31]

Conference

Twice a week the justices hold conferences to discuss the cases that have been heard. The first conference of the week is held Wednesday afternoon, after the justices have finished hearing oral arguments for the week. During this

WHAT AFFECTS JUSTICES' VOTES?

Scholars typically identify four general categories of influences that affect how justices vote: the Constitution and body of law applicable to the case, the political environment in which the Court operates (national climate, public opinion, and so forth), the personal values of the individual justices, and the interaction among the justices.

The Constitution and Body of Relevant Case Law. Justices necessarily look to the Constitution, previous Court decisions, and the law or statute in question when deciding cases. Although the justices may approach the Constitution in a multitude of ways, they all refer to the document for guidance in deciding constitutional questions. Precedents are not infallible, but the justices very rarely overturn previous Supreme Court decisions. In fact, only 122 precedents, or 2.7 cases per term, were overturned by the U.S. Supreme Court between 1953 and 1989.[1]

Political Environment. Although the Court is much more insulated from the public than either of the other two branches of government,[2] the justices are nevertheless products of their environment and subject to some of the same societal influences and opinions as the rest of the American public. As Chief Justice William Rehnquist explains, "Judges, so long as they are relatively normal human beings, can no more escape being influenced by public opinion in the long run than can people working at other jobs."[3] His statement does not mean that the justices follow public opinion polls like elected government officials do, but rather that they cannot help being exposed to the same political climate and context as the public.

Personal Values. The amount of case law in the United States is so vast that often times different justices draw from different precedents and use different reasoning to reach their decisions. It is improbable to expect that

each justice would have the exact same understanding of previous case law, and so their personal perspectives often shape the opinions they write. Scholars find that justices' personal perspectives and ideologies do indeed affect Supreme Court decision making.[4] Not surprisingly, the most conservative justices tend to vote together most often as do the most liberal justices.[5]

Interaction Among the Justices. Justices interact with one another on a regular basis and influence one another through personal contact as well as the process of writing and circulating opinions. At times, justices change their votes on a pending case after they have had a chance to confer, argue, and discuss the case with their colleagues.[6]

1. Lee Epstein and Thomas G. Walker, *Constitutional Law for a Changing America: Rights, Liberties, and Justice,* 4th ed. (Washington, D.C.: CQ Press, 2001), 29.
2. Unlike the elected branches, the members of the Supreme Court do not run for reelection but retain their seats for life, provided they remain in good behavior. According to Hamilton, life tenure for justices would provide "an excellent barrier to the encroachments and oppressions of the representative body." See Clinton Rossiter, ed., *The Federalist Papers* (New York: Penguin Books, 1961), 465. In other words, life tenure is expected to ensure the impartial administration of the laws.
3. Quoted in Lawrence Baum, *The Supreme Court,* 6th ed. (Washington, D.C.: CQ Press, 1998), 177.
4. Baum, *Supreme Court;* Jeffrey A. Segal and Albert D. Cover, "Ideological Values and the Votes of U.S. Supreme Court Justices," *American Political Science Review* 83 (1989): 557–565; and Jeffrey A. Segal and Harold J. Spaeth, *The Supreme Court and the Attitudinal Model* (New York: Cambridge University Press), 1993.
5. Baum, *Supreme Court;* Segal and Cover, "Ideological Values."
6. Baum, *Supreme Court;* Walter F. Murphy, *Elements of Judicial Strategy* (Chicago: University of Chicago Press, 1964); and Bob Woodward and Scott Armstrong, *The Brethren: Inside the Supreme Court* (New York: Avon Books), 1981.

conference, they discuss the cases argued before the bench the preceding Monday. The second weekly conference takes place on Friday, and the justices discuss the cases argued on Tuesday and Wednesday of that week. No one is present at the conferences except the nine justices.[32] If any papers need to be delivered to the conference room, the most junior associate justice acts as doorman.

Conference Discussion and Voting

As with oral argument and during the discuss list conference, the chief justice presides over this conference. It is customary for all justices to shake one another's hand as they enter the conference room. They sit with the chief justice at the head of the table and the other members arranged according to seniority. The chief justice opens the discussion with his or her assessment of the case under discussion and explains why he or she thinks the Court should uphold or overturn the lower court ruling. The next most senior justice then speaks, indicating how he or she thinks the case should be decided. This process continues until all justices have had a chance to speak.[33] The chief justice tallies the votes as the discussion proceeds and announces the results after conversation has ended. Unlike the Rule of Four used in decisions about granting certiorari, a majority of justices must vote to decide a case one way or the other.[34] Although we might expect freewheeling, impassioned discussions among the justices during conference, the Court's heavy workload effectively prohibits such discussion. Rather, the conference is an opportunity to say a few words on each case, take a quick vote, and assign the writing of the opinion.[35]

Assigning the Writing of the Opinion

The chief justice assigns the writing of the opinion, if he or she happens to be in the majority. If not, the most senior justice in the majority assigns the responsibility for crafting the Court's opinion. Chief Justice Rehnquist has said that he tries to parcel out the opinion writing responsibilities evenly, keeping in mind each justice's current workload and particular strengths. Because each justice will likely write fewer than twenty opinions per term, he also tries to distribute the routine and less interesting cases evenly so that no one justice is stuck with a disproportionate share.[36] In *The Brethren,* Bob Woodward and Scott Armstrong detail the role politics may play in assigning opinions.[37] Chief Justice Warren Burger would often switch votes to ensure he would be on the majority side and thus retain responsibility for assigning the opinion. Appointed by President Nixon to bring greater conservativism to the Court, Burger's writing assignments were carefully calculated because he understood that the reasoning behind the decision was as important as the decision itself. Aware that some of the more liberal members of the Court would write opinions inconsistent with Nixon's conservative philosophy, Burger simply did not allow them to write opinions for important cases in areas such as racial discrimination, free speech, and criminal law.

Circulation of the Written Opinions

After the opinion has been assigned, the writing, re-writing, and circulating of the opinions begins. The majority opinion summarizes the Court's reasoning on the case, ex-

plaining why the justices ruled the way they did. Ideally, it reflects the conversations in conference, making sure to draw from the legal reasoning the justices used to arrive at their decision.[38] Lawrence Baum refers to the initial draft of the majority opinion as a "focus of negotiation." The majority opinion often attempts to convince those in the minority to sign on to the opinion, while also remaining careful to preserve the majority coalition established in conference. If those in the minority are not sufficiently persuaded to change their votes, they may also elect to write their own opinions, known as dissents, to articulate their reasons for disagreeing with the majority opinion. Justice William Brennan always dissented in death penalty cases, with the hope that his dissents would someday form the backbone of a new majority opinion declaring the death penalty unconstitutional.[39] Chief Justice Rehnquist and Associate Justices Byron White, Antonin Scalia, and Clarence Thomas disagreed with the Court's majority opinion in *Planned Parenthood v. Casey,* the case that overturned the trimester system established under *Roe v. Wade,* and in dissent they argued that *Roe v. Wade* should have been overturned completely.[40] Other justices may decide to write concurring opinions, agreeing with the decision of the Court, but for reasons different from those set out in the majority opinion.[41] Concurring justices often draw on different legal reasoning to arrive at their decisions, and they write to explain their thoughts. In addition, a justice may wish to draw attention to issues he or she believes were overlooked in the majority opinion.

The justices circulate these written opinions amongst themselves and modify them as they go. As many justices agree, this point in the process is where the real persuasion occurs, and justices have been known to change votes they originally cast in conference while the opinions are being circulated and read.[42]

Handing Down the Ruling

Once the opinion is considered finished, it is sent down to the Court's print shop and officially printed. Before it is released to the public, however, the justices hand down the decision from the courtroom. Justices may elect to read the entire opinion from the bench—a rare occurrence—or simply to summarize the important points and arguments behind their decision. The opinion is then released to the public and becomes the law of the land. The Supreme Court hands down the opinions as soon as they are ready, with the bulk of the decisions released in May and June. No further appeals are possible—the Supreme Court is the court of last resort in the United States. The Court's decision, however, may not be the last word. A decision may be overturned at a later date by the Court, but the respect for precedent makes this route highly unlikely, at least in the near future. Congress can pass a new law or an amendment to the Constitution that removes the constitutionally invalid elements from the original law, but both of these courses are difficult in practice. The issue of flag burning illustrates the point. After the Supreme Court ruled in *Texas v. Johnson* (1989) that flag burning was a form of free speech protected by the First Amendment, Congress passed the Flag Protection Act of 1989, which criminalized the act of burning the U.S. flag. In short order, this law was also struck down by the Supreme Court, in *United States v. Eichman* (1990). Congress then attempted to pass a constitutional amendment to make flag burning unconstitutional. The bill has been introduced in every session of Congress since the *Eichman* case was decided, but it has never passed both houses of Congress with the two-thirds majority required for a constitutional amendment.

Impact of Supreme Court Decisions

The decisions of the U.S. Supreme Court can have an enormous impact on the people living in the United States. Once decided, however, the opinions of the Court have no weight until they are enforced by the executive branch. In Federalist Paper No. 78, Hamilton states that the Court "has neither force nor will, merely judgment."[43] The Court was given no enforcement powers, so it must rely on assistance from the other branches. In the case of *Brown v. Board of Education,* the decision of the Court would not have been implemented without the assistance of presidential administrations. When southern states were slow to comply with the ruling to end segregation in the schools, Presidents Eisenhower and Kennedy used federal troops to enforce desegregation.[44]

How does a Supreme Court decision get carried out? First, the Court relies on lower courts and administrators to read and respect its opinions, incorporating the ruling into their own work and behaving in accordance with the decision. Second, the Court relies on the parties named in the suit to abide by its ruling and proceed accordingly. For example, after the decision in *Texas v. Johnson,* the burden was on the state of Texas to stop enforcing the law. Law enforcement personnel would have to be notified about the Court's decision and would need to cease arresting or fining individuals for burning the flag because the Supreme Court's ruling protected the act as an expression of free speech.

In perhaps the most widely covered Supreme Court decision in recent years, the ruling in *Bush v. Gore* (2000) had huge ramifications for presidential candidates Al Gore and George W. Bush, many Florida state employees, and the entire United States' population. Following reports of voting irregularities in several Florida counties and a decision by Florida Secretary of State Katherine Harris to refuse to certify any manual vote recounts submitted after a November 14 deadline, Gore took his case to a Florida district court. His request for a manual recount was denied, and he appealed to the Florida Supreme Court, which ruled in his favor. Bush then appealed to the U.S. Supreme Court, which overturned the Florida Supreme Court decision and ordered that all manual vote recounts in Florida stop.

With Florida's electoral votes and the presidency of the United States hanging in the balance, the U.S. Supreme Court's decision handed down December 12, 2000, effectively ensured that Bush would become president because Florida was allowed to use previously determined vote counts that favored him by a slight margin. Florida election workers and volunteers were caught in the middle of the fray, attempting to handcount thousands of ballots following the Florida Supreme Court decision and then being told to stop doing so by the U.S. Supreme Court. Although Alexander Hamilton was certain that the judiciary would be the least dangerous branch, as these and many other cases illustrate, the Court's power to shape policy today is quite impressive indeed.

Conclusion

The Supreme Court plays a vital role in American government, but one that is not very well understood. This chapter summarizes the main procedures the members of the Court use to carry out their judicial responsibilities. Chapter 2 will take you through the simulation process itself, reviewing the roles to be played during granting or denying certiorari, oral argument, conference, and handing down the ruling. It will also introduce the two lower-level court cases to be researched and possibly argued before the Court.

Cases Cited

Brown v. Board of Education, 347 U.S. 483 (1954).
Bush v. Gore, 531 U.S. 98 (2000).
Griswold v. Connecticut, 381 U.S. 479 (1965).
Jackson v. Benson, 218 Wis. 2d 835 (1998).
Kansas v. Colorado, 121 S. Ct. 2023 (2000).
Marbury v. Madison, 1 Cranch 137 (1803).
Planned Parenthood v. Casey, 505 U.S. 833 (1992).

Plessy v. Ferguson, 163 U.S. 537 (1896).

Roe v. Wade, 410 U.S. 113 (1973).

Russell/Stearns v. Gregoire, 124 F.3d 1079 (1997).

Texas v. Hopwood, 135 L.Ed. 2d 1095 (1996).

Texas v. Johnson, 491 U.S. 397 (1989).

United States v. Eichman, 496 U.S. 310 (1990).

Notes

1. Joan Biskupic, "Has Supreme Court Lost Its Appeal? In Poll, 59% Can Name 3 'Stooges,' 17% Can Name 3 Justices," *Washington Post,* October 12, 1995, A23.

2. Clinton Rossiter, ed., *The Federalist Papers* (New York: Penguin Books, 1961), 465–466, 467.

3. Lawrence Baum, *The Supreme Court,* 6th ed. (Washington, D.C.: CQ Press, 1998), 200, 203.

4. According to the Constitution, the Supreme Court has original jurisdiction over "all Cases affecting Ambassadors, other public Ministers and Consuls, and those in which a State shall be Party" (Art. III, Sect. 2, Cl. 2). Congressional legislation, however, allows lower courts to deal with most cases other than those involving disputes between two or more states. See Lee Epstein and Thomas G. Walker, *Constitutional Law for a Changing America: Rights, Liberties, and Justice,* 4th ed. (Washington, D.C.: CQ Press, 2001), 12.

5. Epstein and Walker, *Constitutional Law for a Changing America;* and Karen O'Connor and Larry J. Sabato, *American Government: Continuity and Change* (Needham Heights, Mass.: Allyn and Bacon, 1997), 388.

6. Gregory A. Caldeira and John R. Wright, "The Discuss List: Agenda Building in the Supreme Court," *Law & Society Review* 24 (1990): 807–836.

7. U.S. Supreme Court, data supplied by the clerk of the Court, 2001; and U.S. Supreme Court, *The Justices' Caseload,* available online at: http://www.supremecourtus.gov/about/about. html. Accessed June 25, 2001.

8. U.S. Supreme Court, data supplied by the clerk of the Court, 2001.

9. Robert A. Carp and Ronald Stidham, *The Federal Courts,* 4th ed. (Washington, D.C.: CQ Press, 2001).

10. For readers who want more information about the specific facts of the case, the following sources provide additional details: Patricia G. Barnes, *Congressional Quarterly's Desk Reference on American Courts* (Washington, D.C.: CQ Press, 2000); Baum, *Supreme Court;* Carp and Stidham, *Federal Courts;* Epstein and Walker, *Constitutional Law;* and Elder Witt, ed., *The Supreme Court A to Z: A Ready Reference Encyclopedia* (Washington, D.C.: Congressional Quarterly, 1994).

11. Not all scholars agree with the Court's interpretation of the Framers' intentions for judicial review. See, for example, Raoul Berger, *Government by Judiciary* (Cambridge: Harvard University Press, 1977); Edward S. Corwin, *The Doctrine of Judicial Review* (Princeton: Princeton University Press, 1914); and Louis B. Boudin, *Government by Judiciary* (New York: William Goodwin, 1932) for some of the opposing arguments.

12. Baum, *Supreme Court,* 111.

13. Carp and Stidham, *Federal Courts;* Epstein and Walker, *Constitutional Law;* see also Supreme Court, Rules 17–20 for explanations of how original jurisdiction and writs of appeal cases petition the Court for a hearing.

14. Epstein and Walker, *Constitutional Law.*

15. U.S. Supreme Court, data supplied by the clerk of the Court, 2001.

16. Carp and Stidham, *Federal Courts.*

17. William H. Rehnquist, *The Supreme Court: How It Was, How It Is* (New York: William Morrow, 1987).

18. Caldeira and Wright, "Discuss List"; and Baum, *Supreme Court,* 109.

19. Caldeira and Wright, "Discuss List."

20. Rehnquist, *Supreme Court.*

21. WETA-TV, *This Honorable Court* (Washington, D.C.: Greater Washington Educational Telecommunications Association, 1988).

22. Ibid.

23. Rehnquist, *Supreme Court,* 266.

24. Gregory A. Caldeira and John R. Wright, "Organized Interests and Agenda-Setting in the U.S. Supreme Court," *American Political Science Review* 82 (1988): 1109–27; and Caldeira and Wright, "Discuss List."

25. Supreme Court, Rule 25.

26. Supreme Court, *Guide for Counsel in Cases To Be Argued Before the Supreme Court of the United States, 2000,* 8. Available online at: http://www.supremecourtus.gov/oral_arguments/oral_ arguments.html. Accessed June 25, 2001.

27. WETA, *This Honorable Court.*

28. Ibid.

29. Supreme Court, *Guide for Counsel,* 8.

30. Ibid., 5.

31. Ibid., 10.

32. Rehnquist, *Supreme Court.*

33. Carp and Stidham, *Federal Courts;* Epstein and Walker, *Constitutional Law;* and Rehnquist, *Supreme Court.*

34. Justices occasionally recuse themselves from certain cases. For example, when the Supreme Court heard *United States v. Virginia,* 518 U.S. 515 (1996), the case involving Virginia Military Institute's refusal to admit female students, Justice Thomas did not vote in the case because his son was attending VMI at the time. The most common reason for a justice to recuse himself or herself is a financial conflict of interest such as holding stock in a company that is a party to a case. See Baum, *Supreme Court,* 16.

35. Baum, *Supreme Court;* and WETA, *This Honorable Court.*

36. Rehnquist, *Supreme Court.*

37. Bob Woodward and Scott Armstrong, *The Brethren: Inside the Supreme Court* (New York: Avon Books), 1981.

38. Baum, *Supreme Court,* 136.

39. WETA, *This Honorable Court.*

40. Baum, *Supreme Court,* 141.

41. Baum, *Supreme Court;* Carp and Stidham, *Federal Courts;* and Epstein and Walker, *Constitutional Law.*

42. Baum, *Supreme Court;* Walter F. Murphy, *Elements of Judicial Strategy* (Chicago: University of Chicago Press, 1964); WETA, *This Honorable Court;* and Woodward and Armstrong, *The Brethren.*

43. Rossiter, *Federalist Papers,* 465.

44. Baum, *Supreme Court,* 254.

CHAPTER 2

Guide to the Simulation

This simulation places you, the participant, in the middle of an ongoing legal process. Part II of this text consists of two cases that have worked their way through the lower courts of the U.S. judicial system. Each is a real-life case and controversy, meaning that someone has petitioned a court for a hearing to settle a dispute or to respond to a perceived violation of constitutional rights. These cases have already been decided by a lower level federal court and could realistically be appealed to the U.S. Supreme Court. Your job is to assume that the cases have exhausted all possible avenues within the U.S. court system and that the only remaining opportunity for legal recourse lies with the Supreme Court. It is possible that the issues may already have been debated before the Supreme Court by the time you simulate these events, but you should proceed under the assumption that they have not.

One case deals with the constitutionality of school vouchers, and the other with the constitutionality of community notification programs for sex offenders. In Part II, you will find the actual federal appeals court decisions handed down in each case, supplementary readings that highlight the issues and arguments on both sides of the disputes, a variety of related court cases to begin your legal research, and some links to websites of organizations interested in each case.

How the Simulation Works

This chapter outlines the four phases of the simulation and the roles and responsibilities for each participant. The first phase is a certiorari discussion, in which the nine justices decide which of the petitions seeking a hearing will be accepted.[1] Second is the oral argument stage, in which the attorneys for opposing sides of the accepted case (or cases) make their arguments as to why the Court should rule in their favor. Third is the conference, where justices meet to discuss and vote upon the case (or cases) they have heard, and fourth is the delivery of the Court's opinion. The players include nine Supreme Court justices, attorneys (or teams of attorneys) for both sides (the petitioner and the respondent), amicus curiae or "friend of the Court" groups, and law clerks who work for the justices. There is one additional role, the marshal of the Supreme Court, who is involved only in the oral argument phase.

The simulation works best if all players try to step into the shoes of their characters and faithfully represent the characters' views and dispositions rather than their own. Although it is impossible for any simulation to perfectly mirror reality, the better you play your roles the more smoothly and realistically the simulation will run. Keep in mind, however, that no one expects you to know as much as the individuals you are playing. The most important point is to be well prepared and to attempt to make the simulation as realistic as possible.

By adopting the roles listed above, you will be exposed to the personnel, workings, and machinations of the highest court in the land. Throughout, you will experience firsthand the challenges faced by the justices as they adjudicate disputes between litigants, by the attorneys and clients as they prepare to challenge or defend a particular law or administrative regulation, by the groups on the outside as they attempt to sway the Court to rule favorably for their side, and by the law clerks as they assist the justices in managing their caseload. Along the way, you will gain a basic working knowledge of conducting legal research.

The Role Play

To effectively play your role as a Supreme Court justice, attorney, interest group representative, or law clerk, you should research three broad areas: the motivations, goals, and voting records of the nine sitting justices; the motivations, priorities, and goals of the parties to the case (that is, the attorneys and the interest groups/friends of the court); and the court cases and policy issues that provide the focus for the simulation. The following section provides tips for researching these three areas and preparing yourself to become an active participant in the simulation.

Researching Your Supreme Court Justice

To prepare for a role as a justice, each participant should look into the background, ideology, judicial philosophy, voting record, voting alliances, and some opinions written by the justice. One way to begin would be to determine if he or she leans more toward judicial activism or judicial restraint. Judicial activism is characterized by the belief that the Court should be an active participant in shaping public policy in the United States. For example, when the Supreme Court ruled in 1955 in *Brown v. Board of Education II* that all segregated schools must desegregate "with all deliberate speed," it was taking an active role in shaping public policy, arguably exercising judicial activism. Judicial restraint, on the other hand, implies that the Court should step lightly and leave the primary responsibility for making public policy decisions to the elected branches. Understanding where your justice fits along this continuum will help you to make informed decisions when playing your role, and reading some of the written opinions should help you to more fully understand his or her reasoning.

Participants playing the justices will also need to determine their ideological leanings. Is your particular judge conservative, moderate, or liberal? Broadly speaking, liberal justices are those who tend to side with the rights of the individual against government while conservatives tend toward the opposite, favoring the rights of government over the individual.[2] As already mentioned, it is essential that you adopt the role of the justice you are playing and refrain from relying on your own beliefs and opinions while "in character." For example, if you are playing Chief Justice Rehnquist, one of the Court's most conservative members, you do not want to speak or vote as a moderate or liberal. Thorough research into his previous opinions and reasoning should help to keep you in character. Similarly, to write a court opinion from his perspective, you will have to be familiar with his votes on previous cases that have arrived at the Court and the reasoning behind those decisions. (To help you get started, see the "Worksheet on Researching Your Supreme Court Justice.")

Researching the Role of Law Clerk

If you are playing a law clerk, you should investigate the positions and sentiments of the justice for whom you are clerking. Clerks should think of themselves as extensions of the justices, so understanding their opinions, reasoning, and particular policy interests will be enormously helpful in carrying out their responsibilities. Clerks, however, do not necessarily have to be of the same ideological disposition as the justices for whom they work. Although some justices appear to pay attention to hiring clerks with similar ideological outlooks, others rely more heavily on factors such as individual personality and whether or not the clerk will work well with the justice and other staff members.[3]

Researching the Attorneys

Participants playing the roles of attorneys arguing a case before the Court should thoroughly understand the goals, motivations, and special circumstances of their clients. To be an effective advocate, all attorneys should have as much information as possible about their client's particular situation. Playing the role of a specific individual attorney is not absolutely essential to the simulation, but all attorneys should keep in mind their common responsibility and duty to present the strongest case possible to maximize their clients' chances of winning.

Researching the Role of Amicus Curiae

Participants assuming the roles of amicus curiae ("friends of the Court") should fully investigate the interest group or party they will play (see box "Potential Amicus Curiae Groups"). These players will need to craft arguments consistent with this group's ideological outlook or likely position on the case before the Court. Most interest groups maintain websites, and many have submitted amicus briefs on other similar cases that have arrived at the Court. Like the attorneys, the friends of the Court should also familiarize themselves with the particular litigants and specific facts of the case to facilitate putting together the most persuasive argument possible for their side.

Researching the Court Cases

All participants should learn about the substantive issues being debated and decided before the Court. The two potential Supreme Court cases—*Simmons-Harris v. Zelman*, 234 F.3d 945 (2000), concerning school vouchers, and *Paul P. v. Farmer*, 227 F.3d 98 (2000), concerning community no-

WORKSHEET ON RESEARCHING YOUR SUPREME COURT JUSTICE

Name of Justice

_____

1. **Background and Biographical Information**

   Year appointed to the Supreme Court

   _____

   Previous occupation

   _____

   _____

   Previous legal experience

   _____

   _____

   Previous judicial experience

   _____

   _____

   Educational background

   _____

   _____

   Other

   _____

   _____

   _____

2. **Voting Behavior**

   Where does your justice fall along the judicial
   restraint to judicial activism continuum?

   _____

   _____

   _____

   _____

   _____

How can you tell? What written opinions provide
clues regarding the justice's position?

_____

_____

_____

_____

Is your justice considered liberal, moderate, or
conservative?

How can you tell? What written opinions provide
clues about the justice's ideology?

_____

_____

_____

With whom does your justice vote most often?

_____

With whom does your justice vote least often?

_____

Of all of the opinions written by your justice, which
are considered the most significant?

_____

_____

_____

_____

_____

Why?

_____

tification programs for sex offenders—are detailed in Part II. Understanding the ins and outs of these issues will assist participants in preparing thoughtful, cogent arguments throughout the simulation. We recommend that you conduct research to familiarize yourself with the legislative history, legal precedents, and other recent court rulings on the issue at hand. We provide some basic information here, including a list of relevant court cases and some sug-

gestions for conducting legal research. In addition, Part II of this text contains suggestions for further reading.

The Four Simulation Phases: Certiorari, Oral Argument, Conference, Ruling

As mentioned in Chapter 1, the Supreme Court simulation consists of four separate phases. The following sec-

POTENTIAL AMICUS CURIAE GROUPS

Amicus curiae groups for the simulation will be taken from the list below.
Included are groups on both sides of the two policy issues contained in Part II of this text.

Community Notification Programs for Sex Offenders

Groups in Favor of Community Notification Programs

1. Jacob Wetterling Foundation, http://www.jwf.org.
2. STOP Sex Offenders, http://www.stopsexoffenders.com.
3. Parents for Megan's Law, http://www.parentsformeganslaw.com.
4. U.S. Department of Justice, Office of Justice Programs, http://www.ojp.usdoj.gov.

Groups Opposed to Community Notification Programs

1. American Civil Liberties Union, http://www.aclu.org. For copies of amicus briefs filed by the ACLU over the past few years, see the ACLU Supreme Court Watch at http://www.aclu.org/court/index.html.
2. National Association of Criminal Defense Lawyers, http://www.nacdl.org. If no information is available on their website, contact Washington, D.C., office at 202-872-8600.
3. The Washington State Institute for Public Policy, a nonpartisan research institute, has a variety of publications and resources about sex offenders and community notification laws available through its website at http://www.wa.gov/wsipp/crime/cprot.html#cn.

School Vouchers

Groups in Favor of School Vouchers

1. Center for Education Reform, http://edreform.com.
2. Council for American Private Education, http://www.capenet.org.
3. Heritage Foundation, http://www.heritage.org.
4. Institute for Justice, http://www.instituteforjustice.org.
5. Independence Institute, http://i2i.org/index.htm.

Groups Opposed to School Vouchers

1. American Civil Liberties Union, http://www.aclu.org. For copies of amicus briefs filed by the ACLU over past few years, see the ACLU Supreme Court Watch at http://www.aclu.org/court/index.html.
2. American Jewish Congress, http://www.ajcongress-ne.com.
3. National Education Association, http://www.nea.org.
4. National School Board Association, http://www.nsba.org.
5. People for the American Way, http://www.pfaw.org.

---

tions describe each phase and detail each player's specific responsibilities.

Discussion to Grant or Deny Certiorari

The objective of the first step in the simulation is to decide which case (or cases) submitted to the Court should be granted a writ of certiorari. Participants are deciding which cases are worthy of a hearing and which should be denied. To these ends, the different players have varying responsibilities. The justices hold ultimate authority for deciding which case or cases will be granted a hearing, but could not do their work without the participation of the other players. The legal team for the petitioner is responsible for submitting a persuasive written argument requesting a hearing; the amicus groups on both sides of the issue do the same; and the law clerks assist the justices by writing cert memos.

As discussed in Chapter 1, the Court is not free to pick cases out of thin air, but must wait until someone brings a case to the Court requesting a decision. The process unfolds in the following sequence: first, interested litigants, along with amicus curiae groups, submit their written re-

SOME TIPS FOR CONDUCTING LEGAL RESEARCH

This guide provides a basic introduction to conducting legal research. For further information, readers are advised to consult a reference or legal documents librarian and/or refer to an excellent online primer on conducting legal research (available at http://www.psci.unt.edu/King/manual.html).

Where can I find Supreme Court and lower court cases?

Many free websites and commercial services provide full text access to Supreme Court and lower court decisions. Findlaw (http://www.findlaw.com) contains written briefs for the petitioner, respondent, and amicus curiae groups, all free of charge. The Oyez Project at Northwestern University (http://oyez.at.nwu.edu), another free resource, also provides links to numerous Supreme Court decisions and access to audio taped oral arguments. The Legal Information Institute at Cornell University (http://supct.law.cornell.edu:8080/supct/) likewise provides free access to full text versions of nearly all Supreme Court opinions from 1990 to the present and includes selected coverage of historic Supreme Court decisions. Lexis-Nexis, a commercial source that is available in many libraries, is one of the largest legal document databases available. Here you can find the full text of Supreme Court and lower court decisions, briefs submitted by both sides, and additional legal materials. Westlaw provides much of the same, but in a slightly different format.

How do I read a Court citation?

All legal citations contain four basic components. First, the names of the parties to the suit are listed. It is standard practice for the party bringing suit or appealing a lower court decision to be referred to as the "petitioner" or the "appellant" and to be listed first in the case name. The second name refers to the "respondent" or the "appellee." Second, the citation indicates where the case can be found. The first number in the citation refers to the volume number where the text of the court opinion can be found and the second number refers to the page number on which the written opinion begins. Third, the citation identifies the court of law where the case was heard, using standard abbreviations. For example, U.S. = United States Report, the official reporter of the U.S. Supreme Court. Finally, the number in parentheses refers to the year the decision was handed down.

Example: *Mississippi University for Women v. Hogan,* 458 U.S. 718 (1982)

Mississippi University for Women v. Hogan = the names of the parties in the suit, in which Mississippi University for Women is the petitioner and Hogan is the respondent

   458 = Volume 458
   U.S. = United States Report
   718 = page number on which text of opinion begins
   1982 = year in which the opinion handed down

Is there more than one place where I can find a specific court case?

Yes. In addition to the United States Report, a number of commercial sources also publish the text of federal court opinions, along with supplemental materials. West Publishing Company, a commercial publisher based in St. Paul,

continues on next page

Minnesota, publishes the Supreme Court Reporter (abbreviated as S.Ct. in legal citations), and the West Group publishes the Lawyers' Edition (abbreviated as L.Ed. in legal citations). All three of these reporters reproduce the full texts of Supreme Court decisions. The only difference is that the commercial reporters generally provide additional detail and materials for the reader, such as a summary of the case, briefs filed by both sides, and other supplemental information. Because the volume numbers and page numbers vary for each case depending on the reporter in which it is printed, be sure to note to which reporter your citation refers and proceed accordingly.

For the case listed above, referring to the U.S. Report citation, the corresponding citations in the Supreme Court Reporter and the Lawyers' Edition are as follows:

Supreme Court Reporter: *Mississippi University for Women v. Hogan,* 102 S.Ct. 3331 (1982)

Lawyers' Edition: *Mississippi University for Women v. Hogan,* 73 L.Ed. 2d 1090 (1982)

Where can I find federal appeals court and district court decisions?

Cases from any of the U.S. circuit courts of appeals and U.S. district courts can be located in reporters published by each respective set of courts. For example, cases decided by the U.S. circuit courts of appeals in the United States are published in the Federal Reporter, while U.S. district court decisions are published in the Federal Supplement. These are abbreviated as follows:

Federal Reporter = F or F.2d or F.3d

Federal Supplement = F. Supp. or F. Supp. 2d

quests for a hearing. Second, the clerks summarize the facts, issues, and merits of the case via cert memos. Third, the justices read over the written briefs and/or cert memos before arriving for conference, and last, the justices hold a conference to discuss the cases and to decide which should be granted a hearing and which should be denied.

To start the process, a litigant (or a group of litigants) writes a brief asking the Court to take his or her case. For the simulation, the lawyers representing the sex offenders in the right to privacy case in New Jersey and the lawyers representing the Ohio school system in the school vouchers case must write up briefs specifying why the Supreme Court should take their cases. Interest groups who agreed with the legal arguments made by the sex offenders, such as the American Civil Liberties Union, or groups allied with the Ohio school system, such as the Center for Education Reform, would likewise submit briefs explaining why the Court should take these cases. Those opposed to a hearing, such as victims' rights groups or the National Educational Association, in contrast, would submit briefs imploring the Court to let the lower court ruling stand.

In crafting a petition for certiorari, the lawyers should demonstrate mastery over the facts of the case and a working knowledge of appropriate legal precedents and then weave together a coherent and persuasive legal argument that clearly specifies the constitutional issue at hand.[4] Remember that if no constitutional issue or federal question

is presented in the petition, it is unlikely that the justices will grant certiorari. Attorneys often argue that the lower court erred because it misinterpreted the statute or intentions of the legislature, that it disregarded an important precedent with bearing on the case, or that the facts of the case simply require a ruling different from the one that currently stands. The objective for the lawyers is to be as persuasive as possible, to convince at least four justices of the necessity of taking the case. Incidentally, the respondent (the party or individual who won at the appeals court stage) does not usually submit a petition for certiorari at this point as he or she is probably satisfied with the status quo.

Participants submitting amicus curiae briefs should follow the same guidelines and also explain why they are interested in the case. When amicus curiae briefs are submitted during the certiorari stage, either for or against the petitioner, it becomes more likely that the Court will agree to hear the case, so these briefs should not be dismissed as inconsequential.[5]

After the Court has received the written briefs, the law clerks write up cert memos for the justices, summarizing the facts of the case and the legal reasoning used, and recommending whether the Court should agree to hear the case or reject it. Thus, the justices have the benefit of reading these memos before the conference.

The conference discussion begins with the chief justice's opening remarks, if any. Starting with the chief justice and

---

LIST OF RELEVANT COURT CASES

To get started on your legal research, you might look at some of the cases listed below.

Community Notification Programs for Sex Offenders

- Artway v. Attorney General, 81 F.3d 1235 (1996).
- E. B. v. Verniero, 119 F.3d 1077 (1997).
- United States v. Westinghouse Electric Corp., 788 F.2d 164 (1986).
- Fraternal Order of Police, Lodge No. 5 v. City of Philadelphia, 812 F.2d 105 (1987).
- Doe v. Poritz, 142 N.J. 1 (1995).

School Vouchers

- Simmons-Harris v. Goff, 711 N.E. 2d 203 (1999).
- Lemon v. Kurtzman, 403 U.S. 602 (1971).
- Agostini v. Felton, 521 U.S. 203 (1997).
- Mitchell v. Helms, 530 U.S. 793 (2000).
- Committee for Public Education v. Nyquist, 413 U.S. 756 (1973).
- Everson v. Board of Education, 330 U.S. 1 (1947).
- Board of Education v. Allen, 392 U.S. 236 (1968).
- Mueller v. Allen, 463 U.S. 388 (1983).
- Witters v. Washington Department of Services for the Blind, 474 U.S. 481 (1986).

---

different players necessarily carry out different responsibilities. The attorneys or legal teams for both sides submit written briefs prior to appearing before the Court, and then present oral arguments to the Court. The amicus groups likewise submit written briefs, but do not have a speaking role during oral argument. The justices are responsible for informing themselves about the cases to be argued, as well as for asking questions of both legal teams. The clerks play a behind-the-scenes role, assisting the justices by preparing bench memos that summarize the cases to be argued. Last, the marshal of the Court has responsibility for a few administrative duties.

As was true for the certiorari stage, much of the work associated with the oral argument phase takes place prior to the actual courtroom presentations of the attorneys for both sides. First, the litigants on both sides of the case must submit another round of written briefs in which they present their arguments. These briefs are written and distributed to the Court well in advance of the scheduled oral argument, allowing the justices sufficient time to familiarize themselves with the particulars of the case and the arguments presented on both sides of the issue. Like the certiorari petitions, these written briefs should clearly describe the facts of the case, explicitly identify the constitutional question at hand, and explain why the Court should rule one way or the other. Amicus groups should follow the same guidelines in crafting their own briefs.

After receiving these briefs, the justices once again look to their clerks for assistance. Many justices ask their clerks to write bench memos, or "digests of the arguments contained in the briefs and the law clerk's analysis of the various arguments pro and con."[6] These memos serve roughly the same purpose as the cert memos did in the first phase, providing a useful summary for the justice to refer to before entering the courtroom.

The justices prepare themselves for oral argument by reading the bench memos and the actual briefs submitted by the petitioner, respondent, and amicus groups, jotting down appropriate questions for each side as they go. A participant assuming the role of a justice should be careful to craft questions that are consistent with the temperament and philosophy of the justice he or she is role-playing. For example, Justice Thomas is the quietest member of the Court, rarely asking questions, while Justices Scalia, Souter, Ginsburg, and Breyer ask many questions.[7]

Oral argument officially begins after the justices enter the courtroom and the marshal of the Court announces their arrival. As in the conference to discuss petitions for certiorari, the chief justice presides. The petitioner delivers his or her remarks first, but must wait to be called on

proceeding in order of seniority, each justice has an opportunity to speak about the case and indicate whether he or she is in favor of granting certiorari. The chief justice counts votes as they are voiced, announces the vote tally, and then proceeds with the next case. When all cases have been discussed, the chief justice brings the conference to a close. From here, the clerks have the responsibility of conveying the decisions of the Court to the appropriate parties, crafting memos to let each know of the Court's decision.

Oral Argument

After the justices have decided which case or cases to hear, the simulation turns to the oral argument phase. Again,

SUMMARY OF CERTIORARI CONFERENCE RESPONSIBILITIES

Chief Justice
- Read cert memos prepared by clerks prior to arriving at conference.
- Read actual petitions submitted by litigants prior to arriving at conference.
- Read actual amicus briefs submitted by any other interested parties prior to arriving at conference.
- Begin conference discussion with opening remarks.
- Preside over conference.
- Come to conference prepared to discuss merits of each case.
- Speak out for or against granting certiorari for each of the two cases.
- Vote for or against granting certiorari for each of the two cases.
- Count votes of all justices and announce results.
- Bring conference to a close.
- Instruct clerks to alert the litigants regarding the Court's decisions.

Associate Justices
- Read cert memos prepared by clerks prior to arriving at conference.
- Read actual petitions submitted by litigants prior to arriving at conference.
- Read actual amicus briefs submitted by any other interested parties prior to arriving at conference.
- Come to conference prepared to discuss merits of each case.
- Speak out for or against granting certiorari for each of the two cases.
- Vote for or against granting certiorari for each of the two cases.

Clerks
- Summarize the arguments made for and against granting cert contained within the amicus briefs and write up summary memos (cert memos) for the justices.
- At end of conference, alert parties via memo about the status of their cases (whether or not the Supreme Court has granted a hearing).

Legal Team for Petitioner
- Prepare a short, written brief that outlines the reasons why the Supreme Court should hear the case.

Legal Team for Respondent
- Nothing required at this stage.

Amicus Curiae on Behalf of Petitioner
- Prepare a short, written brief that outlines the reasons why the Supreme Court should hear the case.

Amicus Curiae on Behalf of Respondent
- Prepare a short, written brief that outlines the reasons why the Supreme Court should let the lower court ruling stand.

by the chief justice before proceeding. Oral argument for each side may not exceed thirty minutes. As indicated in Chapter 1, the attorneys for each side generally do not get very far in their prepared remarks before the questions from the bench begin. In actuality, accounting for interruptions and questions from the justices, the attorneys for each side will not likely have more than about ten minutes in which to make their arguments and so should prepare accordingly. Although many textbooks indicate that the justices ask questions in order of seniority, the questioning period during oral argument usually does not proceed in such an orderly fashion. Rather, the justices ask questions whenever they see fit and often pose follow-up questions before counsel has finished responding to the first question. Probably the most important role of the attorneys appearing in oral argument, then, is to anticipate the types of questions the justices will ask and to prepare appropriate responses.

Before oral argument commences, attorneys should familiarize themselves with the decorum and respect shown by individuals arguing cases before the bench. As mentioned in Chapter 1, no cameras are allowed in the Supreme Court's chambers, so it is not possible to see video or film footage of oral argument proceedings. However, recordings of oral arguments are available. Participants might consult *The Supreme Court's Greatest Hits* or *May it Please the Court,* two audio collections of numerous cases argued before the Court.[8] Select oral arguments are available through the Oyez Project at Northwestern University (available online at http://oyez.at.nwu.edu). Either way, participants playing attorneys need to be mindful of the protocol observed when arguing a case before the Supreme Court.

Oral argument is rarely known to make or break a court case, but being well prepared and well versed in the matters at hand is always preferable to being ill prepared and uninformed. After witnessing hundreds of attorneys coming before the Court to deliver oral arguments, Chief Justice Rehnquist distinguishes five types of lawyers: the lector, the debating champion, the "Casey Jones," the spellbinder, and the All American oral advocate. With the exception of the All American oral advocate, all other types falter in some way in delivering their remarks. They either stick too close to their script (the lector), fail to respond to the justices' questions (the debating champion), speak too rapidly (the "Casey Jones"), or sacrifice in-depth legal analysis for captivating presentation style (the spellbinder).[9] If it is your role to appear before the Court, you would be wise to read Rehnquist's words of wisdom for lawyers undertaking oral argument before the Court and attempt to adopt the role of the All American oral advocate.[10] This ideal lawyer is well-prepared, thoroughly knowledgeable about the substantive matters at hand, knows which points deserve emphasis, and has an engaging presentation style that allows the justices sufficient time to absorb the argument as well as to ask questions.

The marshal alerts the Court when five minutes of an attorney's time remain. After those five minutes expire, the marshal signals that this attorney's time has run out. Counsel for the respondent then has the opportunity to present oral argument. The same procedures are followed for this attorney, with the chief justice initially recognizing the attorney and the marshal keeping track of elapsed time. At the end of the hour of oral argument, the chief justice announces that the case is submitted and brings the proceedings to a close.

Conference to Discuss Cases After Oral Argument

The third phase of the simulation is the conference. The conference phase is limited to the justices. They meet to vote and discuss their assessment of the cases they have heard. The clerks offer some assistance, as usual, but do not participate in the conference discussions. The legal teams for the petitioner and respondent, as well as the amicus curiae groups, are entirely absent from this phase and have no simulation responsibilities.

The process followed during this conference is much the same as that used during the discussion of certiorari petitions. The justices meet in their private conference room, with the chief justice responsible for presiding over the group. The chief justice opens the proceedings by presenting his or her assessment of the first case. From there, each justice has a chance to offer comments on the case and indicate his or her vote, always in order of seniority, with the most senior members going first. As the discussion unfolds, the chief justice keeps track of each justice's votes and announces the tally after all have had a chance to speak. If the chief justice votes with the majority, he will assign the writing of the opinion. Otherwise, the most senior justice in the majority will do so.[11]

The justices next begin writing opinions. The law clerks again provide assistance at this stage, often writing the first draft of an opinion. Because the clerks are not allowed to attend conference discussions in the real Supreme Court, they confer with the justices after the fact to get a sense of what types of arguments to emphasize. In the simulation, however, all participants will have the benefit of observing conference in action. The clerks in the simulation are not responsible for writing first drafts of the opinions for the justices, but should summarize the points raised by the majority and minority in conference and briefly outline these arguments for the justices. Doing so frees up the justices during the conference proceedings, allowing them to focus their energies on the arguments and discussion at hand.

In the simulation, all justices are responsible for contributing to at least one opinion. If the verdict is unanimous, all justices should work as a team to develop and write the opinion for the Court. If the Court does not reach a unanimous verdict, the justices on the majority side are all responsible for reading, revising, and finalizing one majority opinion that is acceptable to all of them. If one or more of the justices in the majority agrees with the Court's decision but disagrees with the reasoning behind it, he or she should write an opinion concurring in the judgment and explaining the disagreement. Similarly, the justices in the minority are responsible for working as a team to write, circulate, revise, and finalize a dissenting opinion that all can agree upon. If the justices in the minority cannot all agree upon one opinion that sufficiently articulates all of their concerns, they may write and release more than one dissenting opinion. Keep in mind that the majority and minority coalitions established at conference may disintegrate completely or change just slightly as the opinions are being circulated, so all justices should read all the opinions as they go around and sign on to the one that most closely approximates their own thinking.

Handing Down the Ruling

The last phase of the simulation is handing down the final opinion of the Court. The responsibilities during this phase

SUMMARY OF ORAL ARGUMENT RESPONSIBILITIES

Chief Justice
- Read all briefs and bench memos prior to oral argument.
- Prepare questions for both sides prior to arriving at oral argument.
- Begin oral argument by recognizing the petitioner, saying "Mr./Ms. [insert name of petitioner here] you may proceed whenever you are ready."
- Call on respondent after petitioner's time has expired (see wording above).
- Ask questions of both sides.
- Announce "the case is submitted" after the respondent's time expires and all justices have finished asking questions.
- Bring proceedings to a close.

Associate Justices
- Read all briefs and bench memos prior to oral argument.
- Prepare questions for both sides prior to arriving at oral argument.
- Ask questions of both sides.

Marshal
- Announce the following to begin proceedings: "The Honorable, the Chief Justices and the Associate Justices of the Supreme Court of the United States. Oyez! Oyez! Oyez! All persons having business before the Honorable, the Supreme Court of the United States, are admonished to draw near and give their attention, for the Court is now sitting. God save the United States and this Honorable Court!"
- Keep track of time, alerting Court when five minutes remain in counsel's time and when all thirty minutes have expired.

Legal Team for Petitioner
- Prepare written brief outlining the merits of your case, arguing why your client should prevail.
- Distribute written brief to the other simulation participants.
- Prepare oral remarks to deliver before the Court.
- Practice delivering oral remarks and fielding questions from bench.

- Begin remarks by saying "Mr. Chief Justice and may it please the Court...."
- Anticipate likely questions from each justice and prepare responses accordingly.
- Answer questions posed by justices to the best of your ability.

Legal Team for Respondent
- Prepare written brief outlining the merits of your case, arguing why the lower court ruling should stand.
- Distribute written brief to other simulation participants.
- Prepare oral remarks to deliver before the Court.
- Practice delivering oral remarks and fielding questions from bench.
- Begin remarks by saying "Mr. Chief Justice and may it please the Court...."
- Anticipate likely questions from each justice and prepare responses accordingly.
- Answer questions posed by justices to the best of your ability.

Clerks
- Assist the justices in preparing for oral argument.
- Write up bench memos for the justices summarizing the written briefs submitted by both sides, highlighting the facts of the case, the legal reasoning employed, and arguments for and against each side.
- Summarize the arguments for and against the petitioner contained within the amicus briefs and write up a summary memo for the justices.

Amicus Curiae on Behalf of Petitioner
- Prepare written brief, explaining why lower court ruling should be overturned and why petitioner should prevail. Distribute written brief to other simulation participants.

Amicus Curiae on Behalf of Respondent
- Prepare written brief, explaining why lower court ruling should be left as is and why respondent should prevail. Distribute written brief to other simulation participants.

SUMMARY OF CONFERENCE RESPONSIBILITIES

Chief Justice
- Come to conference prepared to discuss each case.
- Come to conference prepared to vote for or against the petitioner.
- Begin conference discussion with opening remarks.
- Preside over conference.
- Vote for or against the petitioner in each case for which oral argument was heard.
- Count votes of all justices and announce results.
- Bring conference to a close.
- Assign writing of the majority opinion, if voted with the majority.
- After conference, participate in writing majority, concurring, or dissenting opinion (whichever is most appropriate based on vote in conference), summarizing the legal reasoning and rationale behind the decision.

Associate Justices
- Come to conference prepared to discuss each case.
- Come to conference prepared to vote for or against the petitioner.
- Vote for or against the petitioner in each case for which oral argument was heard.
- After conference, participate in writing majority, concurring, or dissenting opinion (whichever is most appropriate based on vote in conference), summarizing the legal reasoning and rationale behind the decision.

Clerks
- After the conference has concluded, briefly outline majority and minority opinions reflected in conference.

Legal Teams for Petitioner and Respondent
- Nothing required at this stage.

Amicus Curiae on Behalf of Petitioner and Respondent
- Nothing required at this stage.

are again primarily limited to the justices. Before the opinion of the Court is released to the public, the justices meet in the courtroom to announce the ruling. Occasionally, the justice who wrote the opinion will read it in its entirety, but that is rare; the usual practice is to summarize it and read out only crucial parts. After the decision has been announced in the courtroom, the full text of the opinion, along with any dissenting and concurring opinions, becomes available to the public. Individuals may pick up copies of the opinion from the small press office in the basement of the Supreme Court building, wait until the opinion is placed on the Court's website or other websites, such as www.findlaw.com and www.law.cornell.edu, or access the opinion through a paid legal research service, such as Westlaw.

The players in the last phase have only limited responsibilities. The justice who wrote the majority opinion announces the ruling and indicates if any dissenting or concurring opinions accompany the opinion of the Court. None of the attorneys who argued the case, nor the amicus groups who submitted briefs, are visibly involved at this stage, although they all anxiously await the Court's ruling. Because the cases contained within Part II of the simulation are relatively high profile cases and likely to receive a great deal of media attention, the attorneys and

SUMMARY OF RESPONSIBILITIES IN HANDING DOWN THE RULING

Chief Justice
- Preside over session, beginning with opening remarks.
- Bring session to a close.

Associate Justices
- The justice who wrote the majority opinion summarizes the Court's ruling, explaining why the Court decided as it did.

Clerks
- Nothing required at this stage.

Legal Teams for Petitioner and Respondent
- Prepare a one-page press release stating your reactions to the decision.

Amicus Curiae on Behalf of Petitioner and Respondent
- Prepare a one-page press release stating your reactions to the decision.

amicus groups should think strategically and attempt to take advantage of this situation. Neither side can appeal the case any further, as the Supreme Court is the highest court in the land. Nonetheless, they can use the opportunity to let the public know what specific steps they will take next to further their own cause. To these ends, attorneys and amicus groups on both sides of the issue should prepare a one-page press release that explains their reactions and thoughts about the Court's decision.

At the end of it all, the Supreme Court has declared what the law is and adjudicated a dispute between two or more parties. Lower courts are obliged to heed the word of the highest court in the land and draw legal reasoning from the Supreme Court's opinion while arriving at decisions within their own courtrooms. This is the role and power of the Supreme Court of the United States.

Conclusion

Good luck as you embark on your Supreme Court journey. As you progress through the four phases of this simulation, we hope that you learn firsthand about both the difficulties and satisfactions encountered by the justices who sit on the Supreme Court, those who work alongside them, and the individuals and parties who seek out rulings from the highest court in the land. Remember that the simulation is supposed to be enjoyable as well as educational and that it works best when all players remain true to their characters. Have fun!

For Further Information

Libraries, the Internet, and other sources provide abundant information about the justices of the United States Supreme Court, the cases you will simulate, and the interest groups who adopt amicus curiae roles. Some information about all three issue areas has already been collected for you (see Part II), but you will need to do further research on your own. Listed below are some suggestions for getting started.

SUPREME COURT JUSTICES' BIOGRAPHIES

Cushman, Claire, ed. *The Supreme Court Justices, Illustrated Biographies 1789–1995,* 2d ed. Washington, D.C.: Congressional Quarterly, 1996.

The Oyez Project at Northwestern University. http://oyez.at.nwu.edu/justices/justices.cgi. This website provides background information and biographical sketches for all of the sitting justices, as well as links to cases in which each individual justice participated.

The United States Supreme Court. http://supreme-courtus.gov/about/biographiescurrent/pdf. The official website of the U.S. Supreme Court includes biographical sketches of each of the current justices.

GENERAL INFORMATION ABOUT THE SUPREME COURT

Baum, Lawrence. *The Supreme Court,* 6th ed. Washington, D.C.: CQ Press, 1998.

Biskupic, Joan, and Elder Witt. *Guide to the U.S. Supreme Court,* 3d ed. Washington, D.C.: Congressional Quarterly, 1997.

Congressional Quarterly. *The Supreme Court A to Z,* 2d ed. Washington, D.C.: Congressional Quarterly, 1998.

Congressional Quarterly. *The Supreme Court at Work,* 2d ed. Washington, D.C.: Congressional Quarterly, 1997.

Epstein, Lee, Jeffrey A. Segal, Harold J. Spaeth, and Thomas G. Walker.. *The Supreme Court Compendium,* 2d ed. Washington, D.C.: Congressional Quarterly, 1996.

Jost, Kenneth. *The Supreme Court Yearbook, 1999–2000.* Washington, D.C.: CQ Press, 2000.

Supreme Court Historical Society: http://www.supremecourthistory.org. The Supreme Court Historical Society's website serves as a guide for the public about the Supreme Court. This website also includes information on the justices.

United States Supreme Court: http://www.supremecourtus.gov. This website gives general information about the Court, including its mention in the Constitution, its traditions, how it operates, the building that houses the Supreme Court, and the justices.

CASE INFORMATION

Findlaw. http://www.findlaw.com. Findlaw allows users to search for cases heard by lower courts as well as the Supreme Court.

Georgetown University Law Center. http://www.ll.georgetown.edu/lib/guides/supremecourt.htm. This website provides opinions, briefs, oral arguments, court rules, and information about the justices.

Jurist. http://jurist.law.pitt.edu/supremecourt.htm. The Jurist website allows users to search for cases, read decisions, view arguments, find information on justices and law clerks, and provides history on the Court.

Legal Information Institute. http://supct.law.cornell.edu/supct. This site allows users to search for cases and also provides information about current and former Supreme Court justices, the court calendar, court rules, and other general information pertaining to the Court.

Mauro, Tony. *Illustrated Great Decisions of the Supreme Court.* Washington, D.C.: CQ Press, 2000.

The Oyez Project at Northwestern University. http://oyez.at.nwu.edu/cases/cases.cgi. This website includes links to full text Supreme Court cases, including some with audio taped oral arguments.

United States Supreme Court. http://www.supremecourtus.gov. This official government website offers information about the Court's docket, oral arguments, court rules, and opinions handed down by the Court.

MEDIA SOURCES

Court TV. http://www.courttv.com. This website provides news coverage of high profile trials.

United States Supreme Court Monitor. http://law.com/us_supreme_ct. This website gives information on the Court, decisions, and cases granted certiorari.

USA Today. Supreme Court Section. http://www.usatoday.com/news/court/courtfront.htm. USA Today provides useful summaries of many recent court decisions, as well as a wealth of additional information about the Supreme Court's docket, orders, and rules.

Washington Post Federal Page: http://www.washingtonpost.com/wp-srv/national/longterm/supcourt/supcourt.htm. The *Washington Post* follows the activities of the Court and reports on issues of interest.

CASE CITED

Brown v. Board of Education II, 349 U.S. 294 (1955).

Notes

1. As in the actual Supreme Court, it is possible that the justices will agree to hear one, two, or neither of these cases. How the group proceeds depends upon the preferences of the simulation leader.

2. Jeffrey A. Segal and Albert D. Cover, "Ideological Values and the Votes of U.S. Supreme Court Justices" *American Political Science Review* 83 (1989): 557–565.

3. H. W. Perry Jr., *Deciding to Decide: Agenda Setting in the United States Supreme Court* (Cambridge: Harvard University Press, 1991); William H. Rehnquist, *The Supreme Court: How It Was, How It Is* (New York: William Morrow, 1987).

4. The Court has specific guidelines and rules regarding required content and format for certiorari petitions and for petitions opposing certiorari. See *Rules of the Court,* Rules 14 and 15 for further information. http://www.supremecourtus.gov/ctrules/ctrules.html.

5. Gregory A. Caldeira and John R. Wright, "Organized Interests and Agenda-Setting in the U.S. Supreme Court," *American Political Science Review* 82 (1988): 1109–1127.

6. Rehnquist, *Supreme Court,* 272.

7. Lawrence Baum, *The Supreme Court,* 6th ed. (Washington, D.C.: CQ Press,1998), 135.

8. Jerry Goldman, *The Supreme Court's Greatest Hits* (Chicago: Northwestern University Press, 1999); and Peter Irons and Stephanie Guitton, eds., *May It Please the Court: 23 Live Recordings of Landmark Cases as Argued Before the Supreme Court* (New York: New Press), 1993.

9. Rehnquist, *Supreme Court,* 278–281.

10. Ibid., 278–285.

11. Baum, *Supreme Court;* and Rehnquist, *Supreme Court.*

Supreme Court
Research Materials

Paul P. v. Farmer

The case of *Paul P. v. Farmer*, 227 F.3d 98 (2000) was decided by the United States Court of Appeals for the 3d Circuit in September 2000. Participants in the simulation will study this case and attempt to persuade the Supreme Court either to grant or deny certiorari. If granted certiorari, the case will be argued before the Court, and the Court will hand down a ruling. Participants should read the entire case to familiarize themselves with the legal reasoning employed and to understand how the lower court decided it.

Paul P. v. Farmer
No. 00–5244
United States Court of Appeals for the Third Circuit
Filed: September 11, 2000

PRIOR HISTORY: On appeal from the United States District Court for the district of New Jersey. D.C. Civil No. 97-2919. District Judge: The Honorable Joseph E. Irenas.

DISPOSITION: Affirmed the judgment of the District Court.

JUDGES: Before: Barry and Greenberg, Circuit Judges, and Oberdorfer, **District Judge.

** The Honorable Louis F. Oberdorfer, United States District Judge for the District of Columbia, sitting by designation.

OPINION OF THE COURT

BARRY, Circuit Judge.

For several years now, the District Court and this Court have been adjudicating appellants' various challenges to the dissemination of sex offender notices in New Jersey under what has popularly become known as "Megan's Law." As to one of those challenges, and alone among the Courts of Appeals which have considered *Megan's Law* cases, we found that sex offender notices implicate a nontrivial privacy interest, albeit only with respect to one piece of information—the home address of the offender. This litigation, however, now comes to an end, for we conclude that appellees have shown, in the words of our prior order of remand, that appellants' "interest in assuring that information is disclosed only to those who have a particular need for it has been accorded adequate protection" by the Attorney General Guidelines for Law Enforcement for the Implementation of *Sex Offender and Community Notification Laws* (Mar. 2000) (the "New Guidelines"). *Paul P. v. Verniero*, 170 F.3d 396, 406 (3d Cir. 1999) ("Paul P. I"). Accordingly, we will affirm.

I.

Megan's Law, so named for Megan Kanka, a little girl who was sexually abused and murdered by a twice-convicted sex offender, was enacted "to identify potential recidivists and alert the public when necessary for the public safety." *E.B. v. Verniero*, 119 F.3d 1077, 1097 (3d Cir. 1997). Given that laudatory goal, therefore, this case begins with the understanding and, indeed, the requirement that what might otherwise be private information be made public.

As we set forth in great detail in *Artway v. Attorney General*, 81 F.3d 1235 (3d Cir. 1996), *Megan's Law* "requires all persons who complete a sentence for certain designated crimes involving sexual assault after *Megan's Law* was enacted to register with local law enforcement." Id. at 1243; see also N.J.S.A. §2C:7-2. "The registrant must provide the following information to the chief law enforcement officer of the municipality in which he [or she] resides: name, social security number, age, race, sex, date of birth, height, weight, hair and eye color, address of legal residence, address of any current temporary legal residence, and date and place of employment." *Artway*, 81 F.3d at 1243; see also N.J.S.A. §2C:7-4b(1). Once the information is provided by the sex offender, it is forwarded "to the Division of State Police, which incorporates it into a central registry and notifies the prosecutor of the county in which the registrant plans to reside." *Artway*, 81 F.3d at 1243. At this stage, the information is not yet available to the public.

Once the information is received in the prosecutor's office of the county in which the registrant plans to reside, that office, in consultation with the prosecutor's office of the county in which the registrant was convicted, "determines whether the registrant poses a low, moderate, or high risk of reoffense. In making that determination, the prosecutor must consider the guidelines the Attorney General has promulgated pursuant to the Act." Id. at 1244 (citing N.J.S.A. §§2C:7-8d(1), 2C:7-8a to b). The law mandates that

> every registrant at least qualify for Tier 1 treatment, otherwise known as 'law enforcement alert,' where notification extends only to law enforcement agencies likely to encounter the registrant. N.J.S.A. §2C:7-8c(1). In the case of those registrants posing a moderate risk of reoffense, Tier 2 notification, or 'law enforcement, school and community organization alert,' issues to registered schools, day care centers, summer camps, and other community organizations which care for children or provide support to women and where individuals are likely to encounter the sex offender. N.J.S.A. §2C:7-8c(2). The high risk registrants merit Tier 3's 'community notification,' where members of the public likely to encounter the registrant are notified. N.J.S.A. §2C:7-8c(3).

E.B., 119 F.3d at 1083. After a classification tier is determined, the prosecutor notifies the registrant of the proposed notification and he or she can then challenge the classification through a pre-notification judicial review process in state court.

Appellants in this case "are Tier 2 and Tier 3 registrants who have been certified as a class and whose offenses were committed after the enactment of *Megan's Law*." Paul P. I, 170 F.3d at 399. On June 16, 1997, appellants filed a class action complaint against the Attorney General of New Jersey and all twenty-one county prosecutors (collectively, the "State defendants") alleging that *Megan's Law* violated their constitutional rights of privacy and due process, and constituted cruel and unusual punishment. After the filing of the complaint, however, this Court rejected most of the same claims in *E.B. v. Verniero*. See 119 F.3d at 1111. Pursuant to E.B., therefore, the District Court granted summary judgment to the State defendants on October 29, 1997. See *Paul P. v. Verniero*, 982 F. Supp. 961, 962-963 (D.N.J. 1997). With respect to the right to privacy claim, the Court held that the information did not fall "within the 'zones of privacy' protected under the Constitution." Id. at 966.

On appeal to this Court, appellants raised only one issue: whether the dissemination of notices under *Megan's Law* violates their constitutional right to privacy. See Paul P. I, 170 F.3d at 399. Specifically, appellants "argued that the statutory requirement that the class members provide extensive information to local law enforcement personnel, including each registrant's current biographical data, physical description, home address, place of employment, schooling, and a description and license plate number of the registrant's vehicle, and the subsequent community notification is a violation of their constitutionally protected right to privacy." Id. at 398.

We rejected appellants' claim "to the extent that . . . [the] alleged injury stems from the disclosure of their sex offender status, alone or in conjunction with other information." Id. at 403. We explained that "the District Court's opinion is in line with other cases in this court and elsewhere holding specifically that arrest records and related information are not protected by a right to privacy." Id.

With respect to the disclosure of home addresses, however, we took a different position. As we explained:

> The compilation of home addresses in widely available telephone directories might suggest a consensus that these addresses are not considered private were it not for the fact that a significant number of persons, ranging from public officials and performers to just ordinary folk, choose to list their telephones privately, because they regard their home addresses to be private information. Indeed, their view is supported by decisions holding that home addresses are entitled to privacy under FOIA, which exempts from disclosure personal files 'the disclosure of which would constitute a clearly unwarranted invasion of personal privacy.'

Id. at 404 (quoting 5 U.S.C. §552(b)(6)). We also noted that:

> Plaintiffs' primary argument receives further support from the New Jersey Supreme Court holding, relying on FOIA cases, that 'the fact that plaintiff's home address may be publicly available' aside, privacy interests were implicated by the disclosure of the home address along with the other information.

Id. (quoting *Doe v. Poritz*, 142 N.J. 1, 83, 662 A.2d 367 (1995)). From these cases, we concluded that there is a "general understanding that home addresses are entitled to some privacy protection, whether or not so required by a statute." Id. We were, therefore, "unwilling to hold that absent a statute, a person's home address is never entitled to privacy protection," and instead accepted appellants' claim "that there is some nontrivial interest in one's home address by persons who do not wish it disclosed." Id.

Having accepted the argument that there was a privacy interest, we proceeded to determine whether the information was nonetheless subject to disclosure in light of a compelling governmental interest. See *United States v. Westinghouse Elec. Corp.*, 638 F.2d 570, 577 (3d Cir. 1980) (holding that an individual's privacy interest is not absolute and, therefore, can be curtailed by some governmental interests). Based on the governmental interest at stake in *Megan's Law*, we concluded that the privacy interest must give way:

The nature and significance of the state interest served by *Megan's Law* was considered in E.B. There, we stated that the state interest, which we characterized as compelling, 'would suffice to justify the deprivation even if a fundamental right of the registrant's were implicated.' E.B., 119 F.3d at 1104. We find no reason to disagree. The public interest in knowing where prior sex offenders live so that susceptible individuals can be appropriately cautioned does not differ whether the issue is the registrant's claim under the Double Jeopardy or Ex Post Facto Clauses, or is the registrant's claim to privacy. Thus, as the District Court concluded, the plaintiffs' privacy claim based on disclosure of information must fail.

Paul P. I, 170 F.3d at 404.

In reaching our conclusion, we declined to address appellants' "evidence of recent incidents which have caused serious adverse consequences to" appellants and their families. Id. at 406 (noting that appellants filed several motions "seeking to supplement the record").[1] We reasoned that in light of our holding, "the material [was] not relevant to a determination of the issue before us—whether *Megan's Law*'s notification provisions violate plaintiffs' constitutional right to privacy." Id. We recognized, however, that this court has previously held that 'the fact that protected information must be disclosed to a party who has a particular need for it . . . does not strip the information of its protection against disclosure to those who have no similar need,' and we have required the government to implement adequate safeguards against unnecessary disclosure.

Id. (quoting *Fraternal Order of Police, Lodge No. 5 v. City of Philadelphia*, 812 F.2d 105, 118 (3d Cir. 1987)). We, therefore, remanded the case to the District Court so that it could "consider whether plaintiffs' interest in assuring that information is disclosed only to those who have a particular need for it has been accorded adequate protection in light of the information set forth in the motions." Id.

On remand, appellants raised the following challenges to the notification system:

(1) the Law lacks penalties to deter the unauthorized disclosure of information; (2) there is no uniform requirement that the registration process occur in a setting which protects the registrant's privacy; (3) many counties have inconsistent or unclear rules regarding which school staff members are entitled to receive information concerning Tier 2 offenders; (4) not all counties deliver Tier 3 notices by hand to an authorized adult; and (5) home addresses are included in all Tier 2 notices and are disclosed to all notice recipients despite the fact that this information is not needed by all recipients.

Paul P. v. Farmer, 80 F. Supp. 2d 320, 322-23 (D.N.J. 2000) (footnotes omitted). The State defendants countered, inter alia, by citing various sections of the then-in-place AG Guidelines "which caution against improper disclosure of *Megan's Law* information." Id. at 323. The District Court noted, however, that appellants had "summarized forty-five incidents where confidential information released under *Megan's Law* was distributed to unauthorized persons" as well as "provided many equally glaring examples where *Megan's Law* notices were publicly disseminated." Id. At 324–25. The Court, therefore, rejected the State defendants' suggestion that the Court should "overlook any deficiencies in the current system in light of the compelling purposes served by the Act." Id. at 325. The Court explained that "the procedural safeguards contained within the Attorney General Guidelines are crucial to maintaining the constitutional balance between plaintiffs' privacy interests and the goals of the statute. If, in practice, these safeguards fail to limit the release of plaintiffs' home addresses to those persons with a statutorily defined need for this information, a different constitutional balance would result." Id. (citation omitted). The Court observed that

[a] system of distributing this information with zero 'leakage' to unauthorized persons is, in reality, unattainable. However, the mandate for the Attorney General is not to devise a perfect system, but one calculated to achieve the goals of the statute without unreasonably impinging on the 'nontrivial' privacy interests of the plaintiffs. The record before this Court shows that the current system fails to meet this standard. Currently, there is no uniform method of distribution which ensures that, in all twenty-one counties, *Megan's Law* notices will be distributed in a manner reasonably calculated to get the information to those with 'a particular need for it' while avoiding 'disclosure to those who have no similar need.'

Id. Accordingly, the Court ordered that the Guidelines be redrafted. See id.

Along with its Opinion of January 24, 2000, the District Court issued an Order "enjoining the enforcement of *Megan's Law* until the Attorney General promulgates Guidelines which comply with the holding of this Court." Id. At 326. The Court, however, "temporarily suspended the enforcement of this injunction pending appeal to and decision by the Third Circuit." Id. No appeal was pursued at that time. Instead, the parties entered into a consent order allowing the State defendants until March 23, 2000 to promulgate new guidelines.

On March 23, 2000, the Attorney General issued the New Guidelines, certain discrete portions of which are the subject of this appeal. See App. at 76. As everyone, including appellants, agrees, the Attorney General has gone to great lengths in the New Guidelines toward ensuring uniform distribution of *Megan's Law* notices.

The New Guidelines call for two types of notices to be prepared for each registrant: "[1] an Unredacted Notice, which includes all sex offender information without omission, and [2] a Redacted Notice, which omits the specific street number of the offender's home and the exact street address and business name of the offender's employer." Id. at 102. "The Redacted Notice may include the street name and block number or nearest cross-street of the offender's residence and workplace, but . . . [it] should not specify the exact street number or, if applicable, unit number of a multi-dwelling, apartment, building or other structure." Id. If the offender resides in "a motel or other residence which may be identified by name, the name may be disclosed [in a Redacted Notice] but the particular unit or room number should be omitted." Id. The New Guidelines mandate that only those individuals who are entitled to an Unredacted Notice and who sign a "receipt form" can receive the Unredacted Notice.[2] The receipt form's language varies minimally depending on the recipient. See id. at 153-55. With respect to school principals and designated officials of community organizations, the recipient is informed "that the information in the notification form is to be treated as confidential and may be shared only with appropriate persons." App. at 153-54. By signing the form, the recipient agrees "to be bound by the terms of the Court Order which authorized the provision of notification . . . and . . . agrees to submit to the jurisdiction of the Court." Id. With respect to parents and other individuals in the community who receive the form for Tier 3 registrants, they similarly agree to: (1) "comply with the Order of the Court which allows me to receive the sex offender information"; (2) "comply with the *Megan's Law* Rules of Conduct"; and (3) "submit to the jurisdiction of the Court." Id. at 155.[3]

Once the receipt form is signed, the individual receives the Unredacted Notice along with a copy of the court order and the "Rules of Conduct," which also vary somewhat depending on the recipient. See 145-48. With respect to school personnel, the Rules of Conduct state that the recipient cannot "share the information in this notification flier, or the flier itself, with anyone." Id. at 145.[4] The Rules of Conduct for community organization recipients state that they are not allowed to share the information in the "flier, or the flier itself, with anyone outside of the community organization." Id. at 146. Finally, parents and legal guardians are told that they can share the information "with those residing in [their] household, such as family members," and "with anyone caring for [their] children at [their] residence in [their] absence." Id. at 147. They are not allowed, however, to share the information with anyone outside of the household or not in their care and, specifically, not "with the media." Id. All of the Rules expressly warn that inappropriate conduct vis-à-vis the notices "may result in court action or prosecution being taken against you." Id. at 145-48.

If an individual refuses to sign a receipt form, he or she is still permitted to receive a Redacted Notice. Someone receiving a Redacted Notice is also warned that he or she, along with household members, is "bound to comply with the *Megan's Law* Rules of Conduct." Id. at 121.

Upon receipt of the New Guidelines, appellants moved to enforce the injunction issued on January 24, 2000. This time, however, appellants only raised two challenges. First, they argued "that the revised Guidelines are deficient because they do not require the issuance of a court order which would make the recipient of sex offender information subject to contempt of court sanctions for subsequent unauthorized disclosures." *Paul P. v. Farmer,* 92 F. Supp. 2d 410, 412 (D.N.J. 2000). Second, they argued "that a person's block of residence is constitutionally protected information which will be disseminated without any safeguards against its improper use in the 'redacted' notices." Id.

The District Court rejected both arguments. First, noting that the adequacy of safeguards "is a flexible determination to be made based upon the facts of the particular case and the goals of the particular statute," the District Court determined that "the Attorney General has devised a reasonable method of distributing sex offender information to authorized persons, while avoiding disclosure to unauthorized persons." Id. at 413-14. Second, the District Court held that "information concerning the general area in which a person lives is not information of an extremely personal or private nature. Nor is this information generally within a person's 'reasonable expectations of confidentiality.'" Id. at 415. Thus, the District Court concluded that the New Guidelines adequately protect any private information from unauthorized disclosure and vacated its injunction against disseminating *Megan's Law* notices.[5]

Appellants filed this timely appeal.

II.

All that remains at issue in this case, after more than three years of extensive litigation, is a single issue addressed to the Unredacted Notices and a single issue addressed to the Redacted Notices. Appellants initially argued, as to the Unredacted Notices, that the New Guidelines were inadequate as a matter of federal constitutional law because in ten counties the court orders which accompanied those notices did not contain contempt of court language and, thus, authorized individuals who received *Megan's Law* notices were not deterred from distributing the information to persons unauthorized to receive it. Subsequently, however, the Supreme Court of New Jersey rejected the use of contempt language in any notification order, see supra note 3, and appellants now appear to be arguing that because there is no longer a sanction, contempt or otherwise, they are inadequately protected from unauthorized disclosures of an offender's home address. We do not agree.

In Paul P. I, although we accepted appellants' claim "that there is some nontrivial interest in one's home address by persons who do not wish it disclosed," we made it clear that that interest must give way to the state's compelling interest in notifying the public "where prior sex offenders live so that susceptible individuals can be appropriately cautioned." 170 F.3d at 404; see also E.B., 119 F.3d at 1104 (opining "that the state's interest here would suffice to justify the deprivation even if a fundamental right of the registrant's were implicated" in *Megan's Law* notifications). In evaluating whether the New Guidelines provide adequate safeguards, we cannot ignore this compelling state interest. Indeed, it is this very interest which places this case in a different posture than other cases in which we have been called upon to evaluate whether the safeguards in place were adequate to protect the privacy interest at stake.

In *United States v. Westinghouse Elec. Corp.*, 638 F.2d 570 (3d Cir. 1980), and *Fraternal Order of Police v. City of Philadelphia*, 812 F.2d 105 (3d Cir. 1987), for example, the disclosure sought was extremely limited and the interest which justified even that limited disclosure was narrow. In Westinghouse, the National Institute of Occupational Safety and Health ("NIOSH") sought Westinghouse's employees' medical records as part of its health hazard evaluation [**22] of the Westinghouse plant. See 638 F.2d at 572. The information would not be shared with individuals outside of NIOSH, except perhaps outside contractors who were bound to nondisclosure by their contracts with NIOSH. See id. at 580. We recognized that NIOSH had an interest militating toward disclosure of the employees' private information, but only for this specific purpose. See id. at 579. Because the procedures for safekeeping the information protected this limited disclosure, we concluded that there were adequate safeguards in place. See id. at 580.

In Fraternal Order of Police, the Philadelphia Police Department sought information about certain applicants' medical history, financial status, and gambling and drinking habits. We found that there was a strong public interest in seeing that the Department obtain this information as it was sought not only for the purpose of selecting officers who were physically and mentally capable of working in dangerous and highly stressful positions, but to combat corruption among officers assigned to units which performed investigations in areas traditionally susceptible to corruption. See id. 812 F.2d at 116. However, this interest, at most, only justified disclosure for the narrow purpose of the application process and only to those officials within the Department responsible for the application process. See id. at 118. Because there was a "complete absence" of procedures limiting access to the private information and specifying its handling and storage, we determined that there were no adequate safeguards against unnecessary disclosure to the public. See id. at 118 (noting that "there is no statute or regulation that penalizes officials with confidential information from disclosing it").

In neither Westinghouse nor Fraternal Order of Police, therefore, was the articulated state interest or interests sufficient to justify public disclosure of the private information being collected. Consequently, there was a need for safeguards which adequately protected against unnecessary public disclosure.

Megan's Law's fundamental purpose, however, is public disclosure. The Law calls for the disclosure of sex offenders' information to numerous individuals in the general public pursuant to the Attorney General's Guidelines and subject to the judicial review process provided by the New Jersey state courts. See supra note 2; see also *Doe v. Poritz*, 142 N.J. 1, 30, 662 A.2d 367 (1997) (requiring "judicial review of the Tier classification and the manner of notification prior to actual notification"). For example, with a Tier 3 offender, every parent of a child attending a school within the court-authorized notification zone is entitled to receive an Unredacted Notice. Appellants do not, nor could they, contest the necessity for such disclosures. See Paul P. I, 170 F.3d at 404, 406 (holding that appellants' privacy interest claim based on the disclosure of information to those who have a particular need for it must fail); see also *Doe v. Poritz*, 142 N.J. 1, 88, 662 A.2d 367 (1995) (addressing a challenge to the sex offender registration and notification laws and concluding that "the state interest in public disclosure substantially outweighs plaintiff's interest in privacy"). Moreover, within the Unredacted Notice, there is an abundance of information, e.g., name, date of birth, sex, and conviction, the disclosure of which does not implicate a privacy interest, and appellants do not argue that it does. See Paul P. I, 170 F.3d at 403.

In light of these authorized public disclosures, all that remains is the potential that a minimal burden, albeit a real one, will be placed on appellants' nontrivial privacy interest if there are subsequent, unauthorized disclosures with respect to a single piece of information, an offender's home address. Wholly aside from the fact that appellants do not suggest that, with adequate safeguards, the inclusion of home addresses in the Unredacted Notices would be inappropriate, the New Guidelines reasonably attempt to avoid any burden on appellants' privacy rights by requiring for the Unredacted Notices stringent delivery and notification procedures. See supra at 10-12. Moreover, the notification order itself and the accompanying Rules of Conduct rigorously stress the confidentiality of the information being provided, comprehensively explain how the information can and cannot be used, and firmly warn against unauthorized disclosures. Consequently, we agree with the District Court that "the Attorney General has devised a reasonable method of distributing sex offender information to authorized persons, while avoiding disclosure to unauthorized persons." Paul P., 92 F. Supp. 2d at 414. We further agree with the District Court that although contempt of court language may further reduce the number of unauthorized disclosures, a conclusion it reached even before the Supreme Court of New Jersey struck that language from the orders, the absence of such language does not render the New Guidelines unconstitutional. See id.

We, therefore, reject appellants' initial argument that uniform contempt language is required in the court orders which accompany the Unredacted Notices and their later argument that without a sanction such as contempt the safeguards are inadequate.[6] Stated in positive terms, we find that, as a matter of federal constitutional law, appellants' privacy interest is adequately protected.

The single issue raised with respect to the Redacted Notices is this: the "governmental disclosure of one's street name, block of residence, and name of apartment building . . . breaks the veil of anonymity surrounding one's place of residence" and, thus, infringes upon appellants' privacy interest. Appellants Br. at 45. Again, we disagree.

Whatever privacy interest, if any, may exist in the area of one's residence, i.e., street name, block of residence, or name of apartment building, however, is substantially outweighed by the state's compelling interest in disclosing *Megan's Law* information to the relevant public, an interest recognized in Paul P. I, 170 F.3d at 404. Redacted Notices, it must be remembered, are not released willy-nilly to the general public. Rather, they are generally given only to individuals within the court-authorized notification zone, individuals who are otherwise authorized to receive an Unredacted Notice, but who do not sign a receipt form. Any burden imposed on appellants as a result of the identification of a quite specific area of residence, albeit not the precise home address itself, simply does not trump the state's interest in providing that information to authorized individuals within the court-authorized notification zone. Hence, we reject appellants' contention that the use of Redacted Notices infringes upon their privacy interest.

III.

We conclude that the New Guidelines adequately safeguard appellants' interest in assuring that information is disclosed only to those individuals who have a particular need for the information. Moreover, we find that including in the Redacted Notices information concerning appellants' area of residence does not unjustly infringe upon appellants' privacy interest. Accordingly, we will affirm the judgment of the District Court.

Notes:

1. Those incidents, provided in the record for our review, include the loss of employment, forced eviction from residence, threats of physical harm, and gun shots being fired into a registrant's home following the unauthorized dissemination of notification fliers to the general public and the media.

2. Briefly summarized, under the New Guidelines, when a registrant is classified as a Tier 2 offender, notices are "provided to school and community organization personnel so that they can take all appropriate steps to protect those children and others under their supervision." App. at 109. For schools, the principal signs the receipt form and receives an Unredacted and a Redacted Notice. The principal can then share the Unredacted Notice with other personnel if he or she feels there is a particular need to do so and if that other individual also signs a receipt form. See id. at 113 (opining that "the principal should share the notice with any person who in the course of the duties of his or her employment . . . is regularly in a position to observe unauthorized persons on or near the property of the notified school"). Alternatively, the principal can distribute the Redacted Notice without the need to have the receipt form signed. A similar procedure is set forth for community organizations beginning with a "designated official" signing the receipt form and receiving the Unredacted Notice. See App. at 116–19.

   When a registrant is classified as a Tier 3 offender, in addition to those individuals who are notified pursuant to Tier 2, notification is made "to community members and businesses within the court-authorized notification zone and to the parents and guardians of children attending schools located within the area in which the court ordered notification to the community." Id. at 119. Notification is made by "law enforcement hand-delivering the Notice . . . to an adult member of each household and to a full-time adult supervisory employee or owner in every business located in the area in the scope of notification." Id. at 120. If no one is available to receive the notice, a copy of an Attempted Delivery Form is left, instructing the person to contact the local law enforcement agency or County Prosecutor's Office. See id. Additionally, a Redacted Notice can be sent to all parents and guardians of students attending a school located in the court-authorized notification zone via regular United States mail. See id. at 122.

3. The court orders of ten of the twenty-one counties in New Jersey contained language warning that one who discloses sex offender information without authority to do so will be subject to penalties for contempt. On July 17, 2000, the state judges responsible for *Megan's Law* cases were advised that the Supreme Court of New Jersey did not approve the use of contempt of court language in court orders permitting notification and specifically instructed that such language not be included in those orders. See Letter from the Honorables David S. Baime, P.J.A.D., and Lawrence M. Lawson, A.J.S.C., to *Megan's Law* Judges, submitted under Fed. R. App. P. 28(j).

4. The Rules of Conduct note that "law enforcement will notify all appropriate community members, schools, organizations, residences and business." See, e.g., App. at 145.

5. On April 18, 2000, we granted appellants' motion to stay the District Court's Order and, in doing so, reinstated the injunction which the District Court had stayed on January 24, 2000. On July 12, 2000, after hearing oral argument in this case, we vacated our stay, thus permitting the dissemination of notices to proceed under the New Guidelines.

6. We recognize that the New Guidelines have only recently gone into effect because, as explained above, we only recently vacated the stay earlier ordered by this Court. If the safeguards prove to be inadequate, we do not preclude an application to the District Court for relief.

Background Materials on Community Notification Programs for Sex Offenders

Participants will find the following background materials on community notification programs for sex offenders useful in familiarizing themselves with the issues dealt with in the corresponding court case. These materials detail the history of the issue, related court cases that influence the debate, and the ways in which an eventual Supreme Court decision will likely affect the American public.

Punishing Sex Offenders

BY SARAH GLAZER

THE ISSUES

Shortly before convicted child molester Earl Shriner was scheduled to be released from a Washington state prison in 1988, prison officials faced an awful dilemma. They knew Shriner had drawn pictures and written in his diary about torturing children once he was free, but he had served his sentence and had to be released. Prison officials tried to have Shriner committed to a mental institution, but a judge ruled that he was not mentally ill under the law.

Five months after his release, Shriner raped and sexually mutilated a 7-year-old boy. *

The case raised an outcry in Washington state and led to the passage of a comprehensive legislative package aimed at stopping another Earl Shriner. One statute permits police to notify residents when a recently released sex offender moves into the neighborhood. Another permits the state to hold "sexually violent predators" indefinitely in a mental-treatment wing of the state prison.

Since then, dozens of states have passed similarly tough statutes, often following horrifying sexual crimes in their own backyards. As of December 1995, 30 states had passed community-notification laws. *(see map, p. 43.)*

But the laws have been challenged by civil libertarians as attacks on the rights of prisoners who have served the full sentence for their crimes. In New Jersey, a federal judge has declared the state's notification law unconstitutional, saying it amounts to a second punishment on offenders who

---

* Shriner forced the boy off his bike in woods near Tacoma, Wash., raped and stabbed him, cut off his penis and left him for dead. The boy survived and identified Shriner as his attacker.

From *The CQ Researcher,* January 12, 1996.

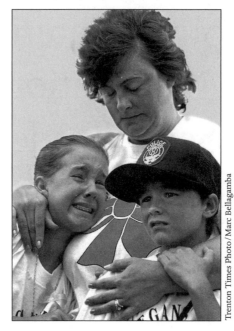

Trenton Times Photo/Marc Bellagamba

committed their crimes before the law took effect Jan. 1, 1995.

Laws that permit dangerous sexual predators to be detained beyond their sentences have been challenged in five states — Washington, Wisconsin, Kansas, Minnesota and Iowa. Minnesota passed its statute in 1994, joining a growing number of states that detain sex offenders with mental disorders who are "likely to engage" in future sexual crimes. The law was prompted by the scheduled release of 54-year-old Dennis Linehan, a rapist and murderer. Linehan is challenging the law as unconstitutional. *

"It's a long stretch from our system of due process and the standard of proof beyond a reasonable doubt to this prediction of future dangerousness," says attorney Kathleen Milner of the Minnesota Civil Liberties Union, which filed an amicus brief on behalf of Linehan. "Conceivably, after sex offenders they'll move on to other areas: 'Well, you're likely to shoplift again, so we're going to hold you.'"

---

* Linehan is appealing a lower court ruling upholding his commitment. Oral arguments were heard by the Minnesota Court of Appeals on Nov. 17, 1995. A decision is expected in February.

The tough anti-predator laws raise basic questions about how sex offenses should be viewed: Are they caused by mental illnesses that can be treated with therapy? Or are they crimes, plain and simple, that should be punished?

The mental health profession is divided over the issue. And there is vigorous debate over which, if any, treatments are effective in rehabilitating sex offenders. *(See story, p. 47.)*

The Washington State Psychiatric Association is among those challenging the state's sexual predator law, under which the state currently is holding 32 sex offenders beyond their sentences. "These are merely criminals," says Seattle psychiatrist James D. Reardon, an association spokesman. "There is no scientifically based effective treatment for sex offenders. We couldn't find any research [showing] that treating is any more effective than incarcerating."

But some experts who work with sex offenders insist they have found therapies that work, among them Fred S. Berlin, director of the National Institute for the Study, Prevention and Treatment of Sexual Trauma in Baltimore, Md. "I don't think the majority [of sex offenders] have a condition that's curable," he says, "but I do think that many of them have a psychiatric disorder and can, like alcoholics, learn to control themselves and live safely in the community."

"There are probably sex offenders who are criminals and some who are mentally ill," says Roxanne Lieb, associate director of the Washington State Institute for Public Policy at Evergreen State College in Olympia, Wash. "It's not black and white, as it's been posed in this debate." Certain therapies may help specific types of sex offenders but have little effect on others who are more likely to reoffend, Lieb says.

"Incest offenders are in a very different category from a compulsive pedophile who targets little boys, has

How States Keep Tabs on Sex Offenders

Forty-seven states require sex offenders to register with local police whenever they move into a community. Thirty states require some type of community notification about sex offenders, such as police going door-to-door to alert residents or posting notices in the neighborhood.

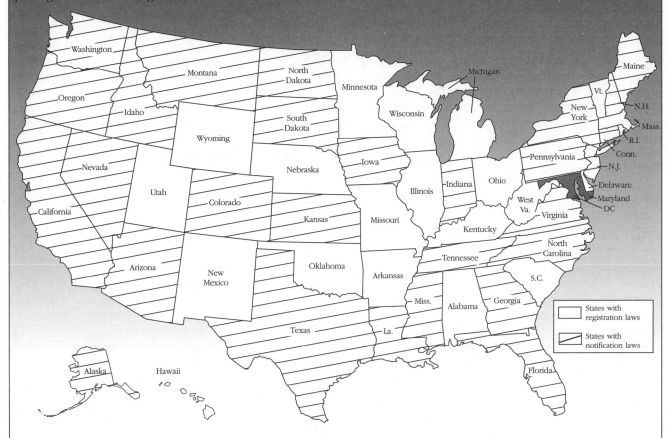

States with registration laws

States with notification laws

Note: Sex offender registration statutes are likely to be considered and passed this year in Massachusetts, Nebraska and Washington, D.C. The legislation has little apparent support in Vermont.

Source: National Center for Missing and Exploited Children, January 1996

done it 20 times and will do it 20 times more," says Lieb. "With an incest offender violating his daughter, it's not sexual drive; it's more typically issues of power and control." Incest offenders — usually fathers, stepfathers and uncles — are also the least likely of all sex offenders to commit sex crimes again — particularly outside the family. *(See table, p. 45.)*

The most well-publicized cases tend to focus on violence by strangers. Yet rape-murders constitute fewer than 3 percent of all sex offenses, and sadistic sex offenders are equally uncommon, according to Robert E. Freeman-Longo of the Safer Society Foundation in Brandon, Vt., which tracks sex-offender treatment programs nationwide and provides treatment referral.

In almost 90 percent of the molestation cases leading to convictions, the children know their abuser, according to the federal Bureau of Justice Statistics (BJS). In almost half the cases, the abuser is a parent or relative. Simi-

larly, adults are more likely to be raped by someone they know than by strangers; acquaintances, boyfriends or family members represent about 60 percent of convicted rapists.[1]

"The public always hates the sex offenders it doesn't know and believes they should all go to prison forever," says Lucy Berliner, research director at the Harborview Sexual Assault Center in Seattle, which treats assault victims. "The one they do know — their brother, their son, their pastor

— they want to have the opportunity to get rehabilitated."

Berliner served on the task force that drafted Washington state's pioneering sex predator law. She defends the law against assaults by civil libertarians, arguing that it's narrowly drawn to get at a few hard-core, repetitive offenders like Shriner.

For policy-makers, it comes down to a balancing act between the rights of ex-offenders and the rights of potential victims. "Is the state helpless?" asks Alexander D. Brooks, professor of law emeritus at Rutgers Law School in Newark, N.J. "Must the state release such a person and say it can't do anything until he commits another crime?"

Initially, Brooks expected to oppose the Washington state law on civil liberties grounds, but he changed his mind after contemplating the legal impasse Washington state faced in the Shriner case.

"Which interest are you more concerned about protecting?" he asks. "Keeping dangerous offenders on the street, where they will commit sexual offenses against women and children, or protecting women and children by committing the most dangerous offenders with the hope of treating them?"

As courts and legislatures debate how to deal with sex offenders, here are some of the questions being asked:

Should citizens be informed of sex offenders living in their community?

In July 1994, in a suburb of Trenton, N.J., 7-year-old Megan Kanka walked across the street to see a neighbor's puppy. She never came home. Jesse Timmendequas, a neighbor and twice-convicted sex offender, has been charged with murdering Megan. Jury selection in his long-delayed trial is set to begin in February.

Unbeknown to the neighborhood, Timmendequas had spent six years in Avenel, New Jersey's treatment-prison for sex offenders, for molesting and at-

tempting to kill another little girl. Within weeks of Megan's death, more than 200,000 New Jerseyans had signed a petition demanding that government officials notify communities when sex offenders move into the neighborhood.

In October 1994, Republican Gov. Christine Todd Whitman signed a package of 10 bills, which came to be called "Megan's Law." The most controversial provision requires released sex offenders to register with local police.

In addition, neighborhoods must be told the identity, criminal record and address of sex offenders who prosecutors think pose a high risk of reoffending. If the risk is low, only law enforcement officers are notified. If the risk is moderate, organizations such as schools and day-care organizations are notified. If the risk is high, all residents of the offender's neighborhood must be notified through such methods as distributing handbills or door-to-door visits.

Although New Jersey has had relatively little experience with the law so far, there already have been some problems with it, according to Edward Martone, executive director of the American Civil Liberties Union of New Jersey.

Shortly after the law took effect in January 1995, a father and son in Phillipsburg, N.J., broke into a house where a recently paroled sex offender was living. They beat up a man sleeping on the couch whom they mistook for the parolee.

Vigilantism is one of the major arguments that has been raised against notification laws. In Washington state, which in 1990 became the first state to approve notification, a sex offender's house was burned down after his community was notified. In the law's first three years, there were approximately 14 incidents against sex offenders ranging from insults to rock-throwing, according to the Institute for Public Policy.

The law's advocates respond that the vigilantism has been minimal considering that communities were noti-

fied about 176 sex offenders during the period. Berliner also points out that before the law the public often learned of neighbors charged with repellent crimes through weekly records of arrests printed in local newspapers.

Catherine Broderick, who heads a unit in the Morris County, N.J., prosecutors office responsible for implementing Megan's Law, says that each notification her office makes will include a warning that vigilante activities will be prosecuted. Broderick notes that the Phillipsburg men who mistakenly attacked a neighbor have been prosecuted. "The idea is not to punish people further for offenses," she says. "The idea is to educate the public as a tool to prevent future victims."

But critics doubt the laws will work. They point to a recent study in Washington state which found no difference in rearrest rates among sex offenders since passage of the community notification law five years ago.[2]

In Camden County, N.J., a sex offender whose community had been notified raped a child at a fast-food restaurant in a neighboring town. The incident shows the bill "is an incentive to get out of town, to hide," Martone says. "It's cruelly ironic that the notification bill is causing people to seek anonymity. It's the worst way to deal with repetitive and compulsive sex offenders. It gives them reason to avoid family, treatment, detection and take it on the lam."

Advance publicity won't necessarily deter sex offenders within their own neighborhood, either, Martone adds. He cites the recent case of a 15-year-old Lakewood, N.J., boy who was raped in the apartment of a released sex offender despite warnings about the man sent to area residents, including the boy's parents. The law, Martone asserts, "doesn't provide protection. It says, 'Here's a picture of a guy we think is a time bomb. Have a nice day.'"

Freeman-Longo at the Safer Society

When Sex Offenders Commit New Crimes

*Recidivism rates vary widely among different types of sex offenders. Exhibitionists and child molesters are most likely to commit new offenses, according to a survey of international research findings. * Incest offenders are the least likely to reoffend.*

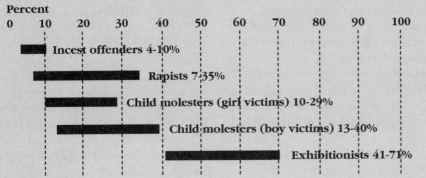

Recidivism Rates for Untreated Sex Offenders

Percent

0   10   20   30   40   50   60   70   80   90   100

Incest offenders 4-10%

Rapists 7-35%

Child molesters (girl victims) 10-29%

Child molesters (boy victims) 13-40%

Exhibitionists 41-71%

* The survey tracked the most frequently cited studies of recidivism by offenders not treated by mental health professionals for sexual deviancy. Recidivism is defined as a rearrest, a reconviction or a return to prison.

Source: W. L. Marshall and H. E. Barbaree, Handbook of Sexual Assault *(1990), in Lin Song and Roxanne Lieb, "Adult Sex Offender Recidivism: A Review of Studies," Washington State Institute for Public Policy, January 1994*

Foundation also opposes notification laws. In New Jersey, some incest victims now fear reporting their abuse because of the public humiliation that could be created by the public notification law, he said in a recent report. "If notification prevails, how fair is it for a child to go to school and hear others talk about his or her brother, father or grandfather, the sexual offender?[3]

"We know low self-esteem and lack of an ingrained social structure are factors that feed into [abusive] behavior," he says. "Public notification will worsen some of the problems."

Broderick concedes that the notification laws "will not eliminate child abuse." She admits, "Quite frankly, for this really to work, it would have to become a national program." But she says notification still provides a sense of relief to parents and has educated families to the dangers of sexual abuse.

When Broderick has knocked on doors to inform residents that a sex offender is living in their neighborhood, she says there's usually a double reaction — shock followed by calm. "The second reaction is a kind of confidence. 'At least I know this and can work with my child and any other member of the family that needs to know.'"

Alerting neighbors means some sex offenders are caught earlier in the cycle of recidivism. In Washington state, offenders identified by community notification were arrested for new crimes much earlier than similar offenders released before the notification law — a median of about two years vs. five years for the comparison group.[4]

Often, the re-arrests are for more minor charges, such as communicating with a minor for immoral purposes, according to Lieb of the Institute for Public Policy, which conducted the study. Detectives in some counties have been assigned to offenders targeted by community notification and

may be giving them intensified scrutiny, she suggests.

Berliner says the law was drafted not so much to reduce crime but in response to citizens who say they have a right to be informed. "If a person who has raped and molested numerous children . . . moves in next-door and you have young children, do you want to know about it?" Berliner asks. "Citizens do."

Should sex offenders be kept in confinement after they have served their prison sentences?

Washington state changed the nation's legal landscape in 1990 when it broadened its laws confining sexual criminals once their prison sentences had expired. Traditionally, Washington and other states permitted the involuntary hospitalization of mentally ill persons considered dangerous through civil commitment procedures. Washington's law was so narrowly drawn that convicted molester Shriner could not be detained after completing his sentence.

But the 1990 law targeted a new class of offender, the "sexually violent predator." The law defined a predator as someone charged or convicted of a crime of sexual violence who suffers from a "mental abnormality or personality disorder" which makes the person likely to commit future predatory sexual acts. Offenders deemed by a court to fit that definition can be confined at a prison treatment facility indefinitely — until considered safe to be released into the community.

A federal judge has declared such confinement unconstitutional because it punishes the same crime twice. In an opinion issued Aug. 25, 1995, John C. Coughenour, a U.S. District Judge in Seattle, called the law "an unconstitutional second punishment," violating the Constitution's ex post facto and double jeopardy clauses as well as the offender's due-process rights.[5]

The state of Washington has appealed the decision and is expected to take it to the Supreme Court if necessary. *

Because Shriner had told a cellmate about his plans to attack small children on his release, prison officials sought to commit him to a mental hospital under Washington's law for sexual psychopaths. But a judge turned down their request. Shriner did not fit the definition of a mentally ill person under the narrowly drawn statute and had not committed a recent overt act proving he was dangerous.

"Generally, the interpretation of [the psychopath law] is they are psychotic and out of touch with reality," Berliner explains, "so our [predator] bill and the ones adopted in the states since then have used a different definition of what is wrong with these people."

Washington's new legislation was intended "to fill the gap in our sentencing structure to cover people who have completed their sentences and are still dangerous" but may not be crazy under a strict definition, Berliner says. There are "people in prison fantasizing about going out and raping and killing children. Well, people [in Washington state] said, 'We don't accept that there's nothing you can do about that situation.' "

Berliner argues that the new law, which has become a model for several other states, was narrowly drawn, thus limiting the impact on most prisoners' civil liberties. In fact, only 32 offenders, less than 1 percent of all imprisoned sex offenders in the state, have been confined under the new statute.

But the law's opponents contend that the state is detaining sex offenders who aren't mentally ill under the guise of mental health treatment. "You can't put someone who is not mentally ill in an institution," says Robert C. Boruchowitz, an attorney in the Seattle Public Defender's office who represents eight of the 32 offenders. "And the state is basically pretending our

guys are mentally ill to get around the due-process problem."

One of Boruchowitz's clients is Andre Brigham Young, a three-time convicted rapist, who has challenged his commitment under the predator statute as unconstitutional. His case will be heard before the Ninth Circuit Court of Appeals later this year.

Boruchowitz argues that the Legislature was trying to find a "pseudomental definition" to get around the rights of released prisoners. "Mental abnormality" is not a clinically recognized term, he notes. And the term "personality disorder," which generally refers to a person's history of maladaptive behavior, is so broad that it encompasses "virtually everyone in prison," he argues.

Psychiatrist Reardon agrees. "These people deliberately decide to commit a crime. To say illness causes them to commit a crime is ridiculous." Though Reardon agrees the behavior is abnormal and may even be compulsive, he asserts, "to say someone who has this compulsion is mentally ill is stretching the boundaries of mental illness."

Reardon also views the treatment offered in prison as essentially a sham. "All the surveys show there is no treatment being done. The [staff] are not trained. The program is not organized."

Boruchowitz says his clients feel more like prisoners in the mental wing than they did behind conventional bars. "It's a maximum security facility," he says. "There's barbed wire all around it. The guards are instructed to shoot anyone who tries to escape."

In a highly critical 1992 evaluation of the treatment program, Canadian psychologist Vernon L. Quinsey noted that offenders being held were "embittered" by the additional confinement and that only three were actively engaged in treatment. He also pointed out an apparent contradiction in the new law. The statute is directed at those offenders unlikely to be "cured," yet it requires them to receive treat-

ment — with their release conditional on a court or jury decision that they are no longer a threat.

The program's lack of any procedure for releasing offenders on a gradual or temporary basis into the community is a "fatal problem," Quinsey concluded. Without it, staff had only the offender's behavior in the "artificial" environment of the prison on which to base predictions of future dangerousness.[6]

Four years later, the state still has not introduced a gradual-release program for these specially designated sex offenders, Boruchowitz says, and not a single offender has been declared safe enough by staff to be released permanently.

"There is no question there have been problems," Berliner concedes. But she argues the treatment program could be improved in the future and that new treatments may be developed to render this class of sex offenders less dangerous. "The law shouldn't be found unconstitutional because it's a crummy treatment program," she argues.

But civil libertarians say the law sets a dangerous precedent for detaining other kinds of lawbreakers on the basis of what they might do in the future. Eric S. Janus, a professor at William Mitchell College of Law in St. Paul, Minn., says a Minnesota law modeled on Washington's statute "is pure preventive detention." Potentially, warns Janus, "The principle underlying it would swallow the entire criminal justice system."

Janus is one of the attorneys representing rapist-murderer Linehan, who at age 24 strangled a 14-year-old babysitter who resisted his advances. Trial testimony revealed that in addition to the babysitter, Linehan assaulted several women before being caught and imprisoned. In 1975, Linehan escaped from prison and fled to Michigan, where he was imprisoned for assaulting a 12-year-old girl. In 1983, at the completion of his Michigan sentence, he was returned

---

* Judge Coughenour has agreed to let the state keep the 32 prisoners committed under the law incarcerated until an appeals court decides the first challenge.

Combining Group Therapy and Drugs . . .

Eight men sit around an oval table discussing their struggles with addiction. But these are not drug addicts or alcoholics. They are sex offenders — child molesters, exhibitionists, a cross-dresser and a peeping Tom. For the most part, they are white, affluent and well-educated.

The men are participants in group therapy at the National Institute for the Study, Prevention and Treatment of Sexual Trauma in Baltimore, Md. In essence, the institute borrows the techniques of alcoholism treatment in making clients confront their crimes while assuring them they are not alone in their fantasies.

"The child is to the pedophile what the bottle is to the alcoholic," says institute Director Fred S. Berlin, a psychiatrist at Johns Hopkins University. "When people have intense cravings, and satisfying these cravings brings pleasure, it's hard to deny themselves." Like alcoholism, Berlin believes, sex offending is a life-long disease that can be managed but not "cured."

The treatment regimen consists primarily of weekly group therapy for a year, followed by another year of occasional sessions. The aim is to make offenders accept responsibility for their acts, find remorse for the people they have hurt and develop strategies to avoid repeating their crimes, such as avoiding situations associated with their temptations. The institute currently treats 130 sex offenders.

Bob, a baby-faced child molester, clutches his coat to his chest as he describes how he recently accompanied a child on an amusement park ride — violating a court order barring him from contact with minors. * Bob was arrested two years ago and attends group therapy as a condition of probation — as do half the group members.

Bob was on a church outing when a parent who was terrified of roller coasters asked him to ride with her 6-year-old child. "I felt sorry for the kid. He had no way of getting on the rides," Bob explains. He insists he was not sexually attracted to the boy.

The other group members are skeptical of Bob's rationale, asking why he participated in an excursion that would inevitably include children. "Let's be real," says Associate Director Kate Thomas, an attractive woman with waist-long blond hair who leads the therapy session. "If the church tells you to do something harmful, it's like friends getting you into

*The men's names have been changed to protect their privacy.

a bar."

It's hard to square Bob's gentle demeanor with his revelations of past crimes. While working as a nurse, he says he sexually assaulted several comatose adults. He recalls reading a pornographic story when he was 13 about a nurse who would similarly "relieve" her patients. "It stuck with me [that] I was helping them," he says. "But in my head, I knew I wasn't."

Thomas says offenders typically minimize their responsibility for their crimes. More than once she has heard a child molester say: "I shouldn't have been doing it, but she came on to me."

There's also an element of escapism in the men's acts. David, a distinguished-looking middle-aged man with a neat, gray beard, describes his recent arrest for hugging a strange woman from behind as she bent over her car in a parking lot. He has a history of "froitteurism," touching or rubbing up against strangers, and of exposing himself.

"I've exchanged normal heterosexual relations with my wife for this," David says sadly. "Your wife is a real person," observes John, who identifies himself as a pedophile. "These people are anonymous."

Though their obsessions vary, the men in the room agree that it is hard to control their behavior.

"I never intended to hurt any of these kids," says Bob, who met most of the children he molested through church activities. "The opportunity arose, and I did it. I didn't have enough control to stop it."

Bob gets weekly injections of Depo-Provera, a drug that lowers the hormone testosterone, thus reducing desire for sexual activity. About one-quarter of the men treated at the institute take testosterone-lowering drugs — all voluntarily. Although the drugs lower sex drive, Thomas says, patients on it can still have intercourse.

One group member, a medical student, was suspended from school for peeping at women in public bathrooms several times a day. He has found the medication helpful in controlling his voyeurism yet still maintains a sexual relationship with his girlfriend.

"They're tired of being so driven by sexuality that they can't do much else with their lives," Thomas says of the men on drugs.

Patients treated with the drugs also participate in the institute's standard treatment regimen of group therapy. In a 1991

to Minnesota and incarcerated.

On May 15, 1992, Linehan was scheduled to be released. Instead, he was committed to a state mental hospital under Minnesota's "psychopathic personality" law. However, the state Supreme Court overturned Linehan's commitment in June 1994, saying he

did not fit the law's definition of a psychopath as someone unable to control his sexual impulses.

Under a new law, passed in August 1994 in response to Linehan's imminent release, prosecutors need only prove that someone is unwilling to control his or her sexual impulses. The

new statute permits the commitment of "sexually dangerous persons" who have a history of past harmful sexual conduct, are likely to repeat the conduct in the future and have a personality disorder.

Linehan was committed under the new law, which he challenged on

. . . Helps Sex Offenders Deal With Compulsions

study of 626 patients treated by the clinic, Berlin reported that five years after they had been treated, fewer than 10 percent had committed sexual offenses again. Among the most compliant patients, fewer than 5 percent committed new sexual offenses.[1]

The hormonal treatment aims to accomplish in a reversible form the same testosterone-lowering goal as surgical castration — which removes the testes. In studies, castration appears to be the most effective treatment in reducing repeat crimes among sex offenders. One study of 121 castrated sex offenders in Switzerland found a 7.4 percent recidivism rate compared with a 52 percent rate 10 years later for men not undergoing the procedure.[2] A recent review of the literature also found hormonal treatments effective in reducing repeat sex offenses.[3] (See "At Issue," p. 56.)

However, Depo-Provera plagues some patients with side effects, including weight gain, high blood pressure, nightmares, cold sweats and lethargy. About half of those who begin the hormonal treatment discontinue it.[4]

A drug preferred for its limited side effects is Depo-Lupron, but according to Thomas, it costs $400-$500 for each monthly injection, compared with $40 for each weekly injection of Depo-Provera.

Because of the expense and side effects, drugs are not widely used. Less than 20 percent of adult sex offender treatment programs use them, according to a national survey by the Safer Society Foundation in Brandon, Vt. "I don't know of any correctional systems that use it," says survey co-author Robert E. Freeman-Longo. "It's seen as still experimental."

Ethical and legal issues have been raised over whether sex offenders can be forced to take the drug. In a 1983 Michigan case, Judge John Fitzgerald sentenced Roger Gauntlett, who had pleaded no-contest to molesting his 14-year-old step-daughter, to five years of treatment with Depo-Provera. On appeal, the Michigan Appeals Court ruled Gauntlett couldn't be forced to take the drug, saying it isn't widely accepted as a safe and reliable treatment for sex offenders.[5]

"There's always the issue of whether prisoners are really consenting or not," says Stephen Huot, director of sex offender and chemical dependency services for the Minnesota Department of Corrections, which does not offer Depo to sex offenders. "I'd hate to pressure or encourage someone to go on Depo and have them say, 'They forced me to go on it, and now I've got cancer.' We've shied away from it."

Also controversial is whether lowering the sex drive really gets to the root of sex offender behavior. Berlin sees sex offending, particularly pedophilia, as "occurring in response to a powerful biological drive that recurrently craves satiation." In his view, hormonal drugs work as an "appetite suppressant."

But victim advocates take issue with the institute's view of sex offending as biologically driven. "By defining the problem as one of sexual preference, and innate, they've tended to argue that the social policy of treating these people as criminals is somewhat unfair. That's where it's controversial," says Lucy Berliner, research director at the Harborview Sexual Assault Center in Seattle, which treats sexual-assault victims. She sees punishment as well as treatment as important.

Some experts suggest hormonal drugs may help individuals oppressed by persistent sexual fantasies but not those with primarily sadistic motivations.

The men who meet for group therapy at the Baltimore institute bear little resemblance to the serial murderers who make the headlines. But they are actually more representative of the majority of sex offenders, according to experts.

"Most people involved with children sexually are not dirty old men who pull children into a back alley," says Thomas. "They're people who like kids, and kids like them." Statistically, the child molester is far more likely to be the child's father, step-father, uncle or family friend than a stranger.

Dangerous sexual predators who prey on children they don't know constitute a small minority of the sex offender population. They're also the least likely to bare their souls in group therapy.

"It's the silent ones, the ones we're not hearing from, who are the real scaries," says a group member.

[1]Fred S. Berlin et al., "A Five-Year Plus Follow-Up Survey of Criminal Recidivism Within a Treated Cohort of 406 Pedophiles, 111 Exhibitionists and 109 Sexual Aggressives: Issues and Outcome," *American Journal of Forensic Psychiatry*, Vol. 12, No. 3, 1991, p. 5.

[2]Fred S. Berlin, "The Case for Castration: Part 2," *The Washington Monthly*, May 1994, p. 28.

[3]Gordon C. Nagayama Hall, "Sexual Offender Recidivism Revisited: A Meta-Analysis of Recent Treatment Studies," *Journal of Consulting and Clinical Psychology*, 1995, p. 802.

[4]*Ibid.*, p. 807.

[5]Anthony Schmitz, "A Shot in the Dark," *Health*, January-February 1993, p. 22.

constitutional grounds. In July 1995, a district judge upheld Linehan's indefinite commitment, saying, "Commitment is necessary for the protection of the public." But the real test will come in the appellate courts in the months ahead. Meanwhile, Linehan remains in a state mental hospital.[7]

"One of the reasons we think this law is so destructive is it puts therapists and courts in the position of gazing into a very cloudy crystal ball and predicting the future," says Janus. He describes Linehan, who has spent 27 years in prison, as "no different from any other criminal."

"What could Linehan do to show he's not dangerous?" Janus asks. "He's had 20 years of good behavior [in prison] and that's not good enough. He's gone through treatment and that's not enough."

Some psychologists say they've developed good instruments for predicting who is dangerous. Quinsey has developed a prediction tool, based largely on the offender's past history, which is "as good or slightly better than short-term weather forecasting," predicting accurately in 75 percent of cases, he says.

But that confidence is by no means unanimously shared in the field. "You can flip a coin and get a better prediction than by clinical evaluation," Reardon maintains.

Seattle University School of Law Professor John Q. La Fond asks how many harmless former offenders would be mistakenly detained on the side of caution. People tend to over-predict violence, he says, particularly when "the prosecution parades the [assault] victims in front of a jury and says, 'Do you want to be responsible for this [offender] recommitting a crime?'"

Can sex offenders be rehabilitated?

There is vigorous debate within the psychological community over which, if any, treatments keep sex offenders from committing new crimes.

Psychologist Quinsey, who represents the more skeptical wing, says most studies are poor and don't show evidence of treatment effects. "I would argue we don't know enough to establish effectiveness," he says. "We don't have a lot of treatment studies with follow-ups."

Some sex offenders, such as child molesters, may assault another child as long as 20 years after their first conviction. But studies may not capture those later offenses because they don't follow sex offenders long enough.

In addition, most treatment efforts are directed at lower-risk offenders — those who are living in the community on probation or parole and receiving therapy on an outpatient basis. "So it's hard to tell whether treatment's making a difference, because their rates of recidivism are already very low," says Berliner. The most dangerous offenders, those who would likely have the

highest rates of reoffending, may get screened out of research studies, may not volunteer or may reside in prisons without treatment programs, she notes.

Complicating the study of treatment is the fact that sex offenders differ so much in their motives and modus operandi. For example, one type of child molester has primarily sadistic motives and seeks out children who are strangers exclusively for sex. Another type shows a sustained interest in an individual child and has primarily non-genital sexual relations with children.[8]

"I think we need to look at different forms of treatment for different types of offenders," says Judith V. Becker, a University of Arizona professor of psychology and psychiatry. She concludes in a recent article that the research literature "provides definite grounds for optimism" for some segments of the offender population.[9] "The majority of individuals who want to work on their behavior can do it, but there is no treatment that is 100 percent effective for everybody."

On the other hand, for the small number of dangerous offenders who have committed murder along with sexual crimes, most treatment experts agree with Quinsey that, "If you're a clinician and treating these guys, you'd have to be a fool to say we should let them go. The data on effectiveness of treatment doesn't support it."

One of the most extensive reviews of sex-offender treatment research, published in 1989, concluded after looking at 42 studies that "There is as yet no evidence that clinical treatment reduces rates of sex re-offenses in general."[10]

But Kent State University psychologist Gordon C. Nagayama Hall says that the review surveyed treatment programs from the 1960s and '70s that would now be considered "rather dated." In an analysis of 12 more recent studies of treatment programs, he found that treatment was on balance effective. About 19 percent of the sex

offenders who attended treatment programs committed sexual offenses again, compared with 27 percent for untreated sex offenders.[11]

Surgical castration, which removes the testes, the body's testosterone-producing organ, is the most effective way of reducing recidivism, according to Hall's analysis of a German study. (Hall's analysis included no such studies from the U.S., where castration is widely viewed as unethical by the medical profession and criminal justice system.)

The most effective treatments after surgical castration, Hall found, are testosterone-lowering hormonal treatments and cognitive-behavioral treatments. Drugs that reduce testosterone, the hormone responsible for sexual drive, achieve nearly the same effect as surgical castration but have the advantage of being reversible. (See "At Issue," p. 56.)

Cognitive-behavioral treatments use group and individual therapy to confront the distorted thinking that leads to sex offenders' behavior. For example, a group-therapy leader will challenge a child molester's assertion that his fondling of a child is an educational initiation into sex.

Least effective, Hall found, were pure behavioral treatments. This kind of therapy generally aims to discourage or interrupt inappropriate sexual arousal. One behavioral treatment lets the patient reach a point of sexual excitement while looking at pictures of children, then gives him a strong whiff of ammonia. This approach gets temporary results but wears off over time, Hall says.

Experts emphasize that recidivism rates vary among different kinds of sex offenders. For example, rapists tend to be the most criminally versatile, repeating sexual and other crimes in higher proportions than child molesters. Incest offenders tend to have the lowest recidivism rates, probably because their interest is concentrated within the family.

An 'Unlikely' Sex Offender

By the late 1970s, Wayne had rebuilt his life. In the small Midwestern community he had moved to he was a respected citizen, editor of the local newspaper and a youth league baseball coach. *

Few people in town knew he had served time in prison for sexually molesting an 8-year-old boy. No one knew he hadn't stopped.

Unlike the serial pedophiles who get headlines for their savage attacks, Wayne says he never threatened or physically harmed his victims. Rather, he says, he built up their trust and manipulated it. The young boys he knew were flattered by the friendly editor's invitation to stay overnight at his house.

Typically, Wayne would invite a boy into his house to look at his Playboy magazines. Wayne would become sexually aroused, leading to oral sex or masturbation. Wayne likens his method to the childhood game of "playing doctor." He says he never engaged in penetration or rape.

In never physically harming his victims, Wayne is similar to most other child molesters, according to Kate Thomas, associate director of the National Institute for the Study, Prevention and Treatment of Sexual Trauma in Baltimore, Md. Few pedophiles "do something physically painful," she says. "Not a lot make verbal threats." Children often go along, psychologists say, because they don't recognize inappropriate fondling as abuse.

Wayne's double life ended in 1983, when an 11-year-old boy who had been given the overnight treatment broke the secret. Wayne was arrested and pleaded guilty.

Knowing that he faced a tough prison sentence because it was his second molestation conviction, Wayne and his lawyer cast about for an alternative treatment plan. A friend told Wayne he had seen the institute's director, Johns Hopkins University psychiatrist Fred S. Berlin, on the Phil Donahue show. Berlin had described his treatment of rapists and pedophiles with Depo-Provera, a testosterone-lowering drug that reduces interest in sex.

As part of a pre-sentence evaluation approved by the court, Wayne flew to Baltimore and entered Berlin's program for three months, receiving weekly injections of Depo-Provera and attending group therapy sessions. Wayne says Depo-Provera helped him control his obsessive desire for young boys. While he was on the drug, a 14-year-old boy attending a class with him caught his attention.

* Wayne's last name has been withheld to protect his privacy.

"In the past in that situation, my mind would have been constantly rolling, wondering if I can work my way to visit him," Wayne recalls. "Now it wasn't. I realized that I was attracted, but I went no further."

However, the judge presiding over Wayne's case rejected his attorney's proposal that he stay in treatment in Baltimore as an alternative to prison. Wayne had to serve five years in prison, where he was not permitted to use Depo-Provera. But he says the therapy he received there was helpful.

At first, Wayne attended a prison drug/alcohol treatment program and was told to think about his sexual addiction every time participants talked about drugs and alcohol. He says he realized the addictions were similar and that he had to go through the same feelings of remorse and concern for others that are the basic building blocks of Alcoholics Anonymous.

Later, in a prison group therapy program for sex offenders, Wayne met other victims of childhood sexual abuse, including a young man serving a life sentence for killing his abuser. For the first time, Wayne says, he realized the young boys he had molested were victims, too, not equal social partners. "In this abusive behavior, I wasn't putting faces on these people," he says. "This was an object meeting my needs, and now all of a sudden I was putting a face on it."

In 1989, after getting out of prison, Wayne returned to Baltimore and attended weekly group therapy sessions at the sexual trauma institute as a condition of his parole. He finished parole in 1992, but he has continued to attend group therapy at the institute at his own expense.

"This is the most honest one and a half hours I have all week," says Wayne, who is convinced group therapy "works" as treatment.

Today, at 47, Wayne looks and talks like the white-collar professional he is. Since leaving prison, he has entered the hotel business. Moreover, he has come to grips with the fact that he is gay and is starting to feel attracted to adult men.

He traces his attraction to young boys to his own adolescence. In junior high school, he had been popular until his family moved away, and he became introverted. Apparently, he says, "I just froze at that juvenile age." Wayne estimates he has abused 75 boys in his lifetime.

Like the treatment experts at the institute, Wayne sees his pattern with young boys as a craving that, like alcoholism, cannot be "cured" but can be managed with vigilance.

"I will always be attracted" to young boys he says, "but I don't feel that desire to take it further."

Most people are surprised to discover that except for exhibitionists, a minority of sex offenders offend again. On average, about 17 percent of rapists commit sexual offenses within four years after release while about 11 percent of child molesters do, according to an analysis of the research by R. Karl Hanson, a senior research officer for Canada's solicitor general.

When it comes to committing other kinds of crimes, "rapists look a lot more like your general criminal," Hanson notes. About 23 percent of them commit some kind of violent, non-sexual crime, according to his analysis of studies from around the world. Only 8 percent of child molesters get involved in non-sexual crimes.[12]

Rapists also appear more difficult to treat. Some studies report successfully lowering recidivism rates with child molesters, says skeptic Quinsey, "but there aren't any with rapists."

According to official statistics, sex offenders actually have lower recidivism rates than criminals who commit crimes for economic gain. In the United States, more than half the inmates in state prisons for car theft are arrested again for some kind of property crime within three years of their release. By contrast, fewer than 8 percent of rapists in U.S. prisons are re-arrested for rape.[13]

Of course, rape and other sexual assaults are notoriously underreported, researchers caution. Psychologist Becker cites one estimate that less than 10 percent of U.S. rapes are ever reported to police. Moreover, sex offenses are often plea-bargained down to lesser infractions and may not show up as sex crimes in official records, Becker notes.[14]

Public concern focuses on the small group of offenders who commit sexual assault repeatedly. Some child molesters may have 100 victims over a lifetime, experts say, but may only be convicted for abusing one or two.

BACKGROUND

Focus on Punishment

From the beginning, American society has punished sex offenses harshly. The nation's first recorded execution of a youth involved a 17th-century Massachusetts farmboy who engaged in sexual play with one of his pet animals.[15]

But at various times in American history, sexual deviancy has been viewed as a disease to be treated. Between 1937 and 1972, 25 states and the District

of Columbia passed laws that permitted sex offenders who were considered psychopaths to be institutionalized.[16] These statutes, writes law Professor La Fond, "reflected the buoyant therapeutic optimism of that period."[17]

Generally, such offenders were hospitalized in lieu of imprisonment. But by 1990, most of those laws had been repealed. "The treatment was not successful," explains Brooks at Rutgers. "Many people became very disillusioned with those statutes and said, 'We'll rely on punishment.'"

In Washington state, for example, a major legislative study on the sexual psychopath program confirmed the critics' view that the programs did not work. In a 1985 audit of Washington's sex offender treatment program, the Legislature's Budget Committee found that the recidivism rate of offenders in treatment was about the same as that for offenders imprisoned without treatment.

Some state legislatures came to believe that offenders were being released prematurely under the statutes, posing a danger to public safety. In addition, some critics charged that many sex offenders were manipulating the programs to avoid prison.[18]

In the 1970s, many states introduced "determinate sentencing," which set minimum sentences for violent crimes. This approach reflected the general disillusionment with rehabilitation and increasing public insistence on punishing violent criminals. In the late '70s and early '80s, rehabilitation programs in prisons across the country were dramatically curtailed.

Washington Gets Tough

Ironically, determinate sentences have now been blamed by some observers for incarcerating sex offenders for relatively short periods. On average, rapists served just over five years in prison in 1992, the latest year for which BJS statistics are available. In Washington, Berliner says determinate sentencing forced the release of rapist

Shriner because he had met good-behavior requirements in prison.

Shriner's subsequent savage assault on a 7-year-old boy prompted the passage in 1990 of the first of a new wave of state "sexual predator" laws. These laws aimed to confine sex offenders who meet a broader definition of mental abnormality than the old laws. If a prosecutor can persuade a judge or jury that a prisoner eligible for release is still dangerous and suffers from a mental disorder, the prisoner can be detained until the state determines he is rehabilitated.

The Washington statute was part of a broad law aimed at sex offenders, known as the Community Protection Act. Another pioneering statute in the act requires communities to be notified about newly released sexual offenders in the area. Components of the comprehensive Washington legislation that have received less national attention, but which Berliner considers equally important, include:

- Treating victims of sexual assault and children with sexual behavior problems;
- Treating juvenile sex offenders; and
- Establishing standards for professionals who treat sex offenders.

Since 1990, several states have used Washington's predator statute as a model, including Minnesota, Kansas, California, Arizona and Nevada. Law Professor Janus believes that the laws have sprung up largely in response to public sentiment that sentences are generally too short for violent offenders.

La Fond says the new trend toward involuntary therapy for sexual offenders recalls the thinking behind the early psychopath laws, when it was widely believed that sexual deviancy was a treatable illness. "You're getting a resurgence from the psychology camp saying, 'This may not be mental illness, but it's a behavioral problem.'"

Child Abuse Reporting Laws

In the 1960s and '70s, growing

Continued on p. 53

Chronology

1930s *In an era optimistic about the powers of psychotherapy, states begin passing laws permitting involuntary commitment of sex criminals to mental hospitals in lieu of prison.*

1937
Minnesota becomes one of the first states to enact a "sexual psychopath" law, authorizing the government to place a sex offender in a psychiatric institution for treatment instead of prison.

1960s *By the late 1960s, well over half the states have enacted "sexual psychopath" laws permitting the state to commit sex criminals indefinitely for mental treatment. Federal government pushes states to adopt laws requiring reporting of child abuse.*

1963
U.S. Children's Bureau drafts model legislation for states to require physicians to report suspected child abuse. Within three years, all states enact reporting laws.

1970s *Crime increases at alarming rates, raising questions about the goal of rehabilitation for criminals. Between 1971 and 1980, the violent crime rate increases almost 50 percent, according to the FBI. Rise in reported cases of child abuse prompts academic studies and the first federal abuse legislation.*

1974
President Richard M. Nixon signs Child Abuse Prevention and Treatment Act establishing federal Center on Child Abuse and Neglect.

1980s *As the national mood turns away from criminal rehabilitation and toward punishment, states begin repealing their sexual psychopath laws and adopting "determinate sentencing" laws to ensure prison sentences for violent crimes. All but a handful of states repeal their sexual psychopath laws by 1990.*

1981
California Legislature repeals its Mentally Disordered Sex Offender legislation, stating that sex offenses are not the product of "mental disease."

1984
Washington state passes legislation phasing out its sexual psychopath law and adopting a determinate-sentencing scheme.

1989
Psychologist Lita Furby publishes review of 42 treatment studies finding no evidence that clinical treatment reduces recidivism among sex offenders.

1990s *Responding to crimes committed by released sex offenders with histories of violent sexual assault, states pass laws to detain sex offenders longer for mental treatment and to warn communities about released sex offenders.*

1990
Washington passes pioneering Community Protection Act, permitting the state to detain dangerous "sexual predators" in mental treatment indefinitely after their prison sentences expire.

1994
President Clinton signs federal crime bill urging states to pass sex offender registration statutes by 1997 and encouraging passage of community notification laws.

October 1994
Following the murder of 7-year-old Megan Kanka, allegedly by a released sex criminal, New Jersey enacts "Megan's Law" requiring communities to be notified about dangerous sex offenders who move into the area; it is considered the toughest law of its kind.

Feb. 28, 1995
A federal judge in Newark, N.J., declares the notification provision of "Megan's Law" unconstitutional. The state is appealing the case, which is expected to reach the U.S. Supreme Court.

Aug. 25, 1995
A federal judge declares Washington state's sexual predator law unconstitutional on the grounds that it punishes the same crime twice. The state is appealing the decision, which is also expected to reach the Supreme Court.

Continued from p. 51

awareness of child abuse prompted the federal government to pass legislation encouraging the reporting of such offenses. In 1964, the U.S. Children's Bureau drafted model legislation requiring physicians to report suspected child abuse. Within three years, all states had enacted such reporting laws.[19]

Some of these laws had the unintended effect of driving sex offenders underground, some treatment experts charge. For example, in 1988, Maryland expanded its reporting law to require treatment professionals to report disclosures by adult patients about their abuse of children while they were in treatment. In 1989, all patient disclosures, even about abuse that occurred before treatment, became reportable in Maryland.

Since the reporting change in 1989, the number of adult patients voluntarily coming to the Johns Hopkins University Sexual Disorders Clinic (now the National Institute for the Study, Prevention and Treatment of Sexual Trauma) has dropped from approximately seven per year to zero, according to clinic Director Berlin.

"The law that's intended to make society safer is actually deterring undetected people with pedophilia from getting treatment that would enable them to be less risk to the community," Berlin says.

The 'Typical' Offender

Sex offenders come from all classes of society. But in contrast to most criminals, those in state prisons for rape or sexual assault are "primarily older white males," notes Allen J. Beck, a BJS statistician.

Unlike youths arrested for stealing cars or TV sets, whose criminal activity usually decreases as they age, sex offenders can be remarkably persistent. While sex offenders account for only one out of 10 state prison inmates, they represent one of every four prisoners over age 54, Beck says.

Nevertheless, treatment experts say

Reginald Muldrew, also known as the "pillowcase rapist," was released from a California prison in December 1995.

it is becoming increasingly clear that most adult offenders commit their first sexual crimes before reaching adulthood. According to one study, 60-80 percent of adult sex offenders began their deviant behavior as teenagers.[20]

In one national study of 1,600 youths referred to treatment programs, sexual offenders ranged in age from 5-19, with a median age between 14 and 15. Over 90 percent of the juvenile offenders had victimized a relative or acquaintance. The most common scenario involved a victim age 7 or 8.[21]

Numerous theories explain why people become sex offenders. They range from the biological — offenders have higher testosterone levels and thus stronger sex drives — to the environmental. Freeman-Longo at the Safer

Society Foundation says the children and teens he sees have been victims of childhood abuse themselves. "We see kids 4-6 who have been sexually abused. They act it out on other kids at the same ages."

"A lot of these kids are masturbating to thoughts of sexually abusing and molesting people," says Freeman-Longo. "We believe this behavior in most cases is learned, and we believe we can help them unlearn the behavior."

Another theory views sex offenders, especially pedophiles, as never having acquired the social skills necessary for normal adult relationships. In American society, "we have a very definite pressure for people to succeed socially," Freeman-Longo says. "For someone who comes up short," a less threatening form of behavior, like a relationship with a child or flashing in front of strangers, "is an option." ∎

CURRENT SITUATION

Tracking Offenders

Despite statistics indicating that many sex criminals do not repeat their crimes, the public is not convinced. Over the past three years, as a result, states have been busy enacting a variety of laws to track sex offenders after they leave prison. As of November 1995, 47 states had laws requiring offenders to register with law enforcement authorities whenever they move into a community; in 1993, only 24 states had such registration laws.

Generally, these laws require offenders to provide their name, address, place of employment and sex convictions for up to 10 years after leaving prison. In most states, the registration information is available only to police. Registration helps police enforce court orders forbidding child molesters from working around children — such as in day-care centers or nursery schools. It also gives police a headstart if, for example, a parent calls with concerns about a neighbor who happens to be registered, according to Teresa Klingensmith, manager of legislative affairs at the National Center for Missing and Exploited Children in Arlington, Va.

"With registration, police can say, 'Ma'am, it's probably not a good idea for your child to be alone with this individual,'" even though they can't give explicit information, Klingensmith says. "Meanwhile, they send a squad car to check things out."

The 1994 omnibus anti-crime bill gave states additional impetus to enact registration laws. States that don't pass them by 1997 lose a portion of their federal crime-fighting funds under the sweeping $30.2 billion legislation. The law also encourages the state to enact community notification laws.[22]

Notification Laws

As of December 1995, 30 states had gone a step further, passing laws requiring communities to be notified about dangerous sex offenders. Both registration and notification laws have been challenged in the courts. Though some decisions have limited the scope of registration laws, they have generally withstood constitutional challenges. The legal status of the notification laws is less clear.

New Jersey's notification law has been challenged on constitutional grounds. Because of lower-court rulings halting the notifications, the state has had barely six weeks of experience with the law since it took effect Jan. 1, 1995. New Jersey's Supreme Court

---

In 1980, 20,500 men and women were in state prisons for sex offenses. By 1993, the number had quadrupled to 80,000, growing faster than the general prison population, which tripled in the same period, according to the Bureau of Justice Statistics.

---

ruled in July 1995 that the law was constitutional but ordered the state to give sex offenders more due-process rights, including the right to appeal their notification status before a judge. New Jersey prosecutors were preparing to resume enforcing the law again under the new procedures in December.

Meanwhile, a federal district court judge in Newark has declared the notification law unconstitutional because of its retroactive nature. New Jersey's law, the nation's toughest, covers anyone who has ever, at any time, committed a sex crime. (Washington state's law, by contrast, applies only to offenders about to be released or on probation or parole.)

However, the New Jersey Supreme Court decision upholding the statute takes precedence, and thus the notification law remains enforceable pending resolution of the appeals in federal courts. But most experts agree the constitutional questions will cast a shadow over such laws until the issue is eventually resolved by the United States Supreme Court.

The challenge to the law in federal court was brought by a man who was found guilty of sodomy in 1971 and sentenced to 20 years in state prison. After his release, Megan's Law was enacted and applied retroactively to him. The man, Alexander Artway, argued that because he had already served his time, community notification amounted to a second punishment.

Federal District Judge Nicholas H. Politan found that the law violated the U.S. Constitution's ex post facto clause, which forbids laws that change the punishment attached to a crime after the crime has been committed. He likened the notification law to the "Scarlet Letter" in Colonial America and the Star of David that Jews were forced to wear in Nazi Germany. Public notification could affect an individual's ability to be employed and to return to a normal, law-abiding life in the community, the judge said, thus constituting a second punishment.[23]

"The judge is saying, 'You didn't tell people [about notification] when they pleaded guilty two decades ago, and so it's unfair to say now, 'Here's another punishment,'" says Martone of the ACLU, which filed an amicus brief challenging the law.

The state of New Jersey has appealed the federal decision to the Third Circuit, arguing that the notification is merely regulatory, not a punishment. A decision is expected early this year. The losing side is expected to appeal to the Supreme Court.

In addition to its constitutional problems, New Jersey's law faces a practical hurdle. Some 2,100 sex offenders have registered so far, but the number eligible could be in the tens of thousands. "One of the failures is the only way notification works is if you have a universe of honest, compliant sex offenders," says Martone.

But sex offenders have been inventive in evading the laws. In Washington state, offenders have given vacant lots as their addresses. In New Jersey, released prisoners have embarrassed innocent citizens by giving their addresses.

Klingensmith estimates that 15 states have followed Washington state in enacting sexual predator laws permitting violent and mentally ill offenders to be held for treatment after completing their prison sentences. The constitutionality of such laws has been challenged in five states. Most eyes are trained on Washington state, which has appealed a federal ruling that the law is unconstitutional. Oral arguments are set for March in the Ninth Circuit Court of Appeals.

Harsher Sentences

Harsher sentences being meted out today reflect the increased public anxiety over violent sex crimes. Reported rapes, for example, grew by 14 percent between 1988 and 1994. But experts say the main reason for the harsher sentences (and resulting rise in the prison population) is that judges are doing what the public wants — locking up sex criminals for longer periods.

In 1980, 20,500 men and women were in state prisons for sex offenses. By 1993, the number had quadrupled to 80,000, growing faster than the general prison population, which tripled in the same period, according to the BJS.

Between 1988 and 1992, the average time rapists served in prison rose from 48 months to 57 months. On average,

rapists served 50.4 percent of their sentences, while first-time murderers went free after serving only 41 percent of their sentences.[24]

The numbers disguise the fact that sentences are all over the board for sex offenders. In some states, a molester with numerous victims may get just four years; in others the same offender may receive 20 years, according to the Center for Missing Children.

At the same time, funding for treatment in prisons has been drying up. In the past year, Alabama, Virginia, Oregon and California have shut down their programs, according to the Safer Society Foundation. "Most sex offenders in prison do not get treatment," says Freeman- Longo. "You have to go to private clinics, and not every state has one."

One reason for the closed programs is expense. In Washington, institutionalized sex offenders cost the state $100,000 per person annually, about four times the cost of regular imprisonment. Another reason is undoubtedly the current get-tough-on-crime climate. "Since politicians are unwilling to pay for treatment in prison, there's very little rehabilitation," says Klingensmith. "The public is thinking, 'Let's just incapacitate them.'"

Treatment Approaches

In a 1994 national survey, the Safer Society Foundation counted 1,784 public and private sex-offender treatment programs nationwide, 710 of them for adults. The most popular single treatment approach is the behavioral-cognitive approach, which seeks to change sex offenders' warped thinking about their crimes through such means as group therapy. The next most popular approach, known as relapse prevention, combines therapy for sex offenders with monitoring by counselors trained to recognize when offenders are falling into

old behavior patterns.[25]

The nation's most extensive relapse prevention program, set up in Arizona in 1987, allows lifelong probation for sex offenders considered likely to reoffend. According to psychologist Becker, virtually all convicted child molesters in the state are put into the program — either instead of prison or upon release from prison for a second molestation conviction. Participants must attend two hours of outpatient group therapy per week for at least 18 months. Probation officers and specially trained "surveillance" officers make unannounced visits to those probationers considered most likely to commit another crime.[26]

Arizona is the only state with lifelong probation. But the idea of using probation and parole with mandated treatment as an alternative to prison is becoming "more and more common" nationwide, according to Freeman-Longo. Part of the motivation is avoiding the cost and overcrowding of prisons.

"We can't put everyone that commits a crime in prison," says probation officer Randy Walker, who works with sex offenders in Maricopa County, Ariz. "Otherwise we'd have to put a chain-link fence around Arizona." Arizona's toughened probation program, including mandatory therapy, costs the state $3,500 per individual annually, compared to $16,000 for keeping a prisoner behind bars, according to Lori Scott, supervisor of the sex offender unit for Maricopa County Adult Probation in Phoenix.

Under the Arizona law, lifetime probationers must meet 17 conditions on their lifestyle, including living at an approved residence, generally one not located near a school or playground, and are generally prohibited from dating women with children, possessing pornographic material or patronizing topless bars or adult bookstores.

In Arizona, a sex offender who violates any of these conditions can have his probation revoked and be

Continued on p. 57

At Issue:

Is 'chemical castration' an acceptable way to treat sex offenders?

DOUGLAS J. BESHAROV
Resident scholar, American Enterprise Institute.

FROM *ABA JOURNAL*, JULY 1992.

On humanitarian and civil liberties grounds, most experts now oppose [surgical castration] and it is unlikely that many courts will turn to it as an alternative to incarceration — especially since there is a better option.

First tried more than 25 years ago, the use of hormone suppressors — also known as "chemical castration" — has proven highly effective for certain sex offenders. The most common drug used is medroxyprogesterone acetate, a synthetic progesterone originally developed as a contraceptive marketed as Depo-Provera. . . .

Carefully conducted research indicates that hormone therapy works — when coupled with appropriate counseling — for most paraphiliacs (sex offenders driven by overwhelming sexual fantasies). Recidivism rates are under 5 percent.

Just as in surgical castration, the subject can still have erections, and many successfully impregnate their wives. For this reason, hormone treatment does not work for anti-social personalities or for those whose sex offenses are motivated by feelings of anger, violence or power. The treatment does not reach the causes of their harmful behavior. Thus, proper diagnosis is essential.

Some may argue that hormone treatment as an alternative to incarceration is too lenient for serious sex crimes. First, it is possible to combine treatment with incarceration. But more importantly, we should remember how frequently serious offenders serve very short sentences. Nationally, convicted rapists serve less than six years in jail, and that does not include all those who plead guilty to a lesser offense. For too many offenders, the sexual abuse and violence in prisons merely heightens their propensity to commit further crimes. . . .

Others will oppose using these drugs because, even though they work, they are an invasion of bodily integrity and reproductive freedom. (Side effects include weight gain, hot flashes and hypertension.) But it is more accurate to see them as equivalent to the psychotropic drugs, which include antidepressants, antipsychotics and tranquilizers, now routinely used to treat many mental disorders.

Some would even deny defendants the right to accept the treatment in lieu of imprisonment because the choice is inherently coercive. Perhaps it is. But the question is this: When faced with the certainty of incarceration, wouldn't we all want to be able to make such a choice? To ask the question is to answer it.

After all the sensationalism, the use of hormone-suppressing drugs, in certain cases, holds great promise for reducing the level of sexual violence against women and children. As a voluntary alternative, it is in both the defendant's and society's interest.

ANDREW VACHSS
Juvenile justice advocate and crime novelist.

FROM *ABA JOURNAL*, JULY 1992.

As a criminal justice response to the chronic, dangerous sexual psychopath, castration of any kind is morally pernicious and pragmatically impotent. Even if we could ignore the implications of mutilation-as-compensation for criminal offenses, castration must be rejected on the most essential of grounds: The "cure" will exacerbate the "disease." . . .

Violent sex offenders are not victims of their heightened sex drives. Rapists may be "expressing their rage." Predatory pedophiles may be "replaying their old scripts." But any sexual sadist, properly interviewed, will tell you the truth: They do what they do because they want to do it. Their behavior is not the product of sickness — it is volitional.

Castration will not remove the source of a violent sex offender's rage — only one single instrument of its expression. . . . The castration remedy implies some biological cause for sexual offenses. Once fixed, the offender ceases to be a danger. This is nonsense — the motivation for sexual assault will not disappear with the severed genitalia or altered hormones. . . .

Even the most liberal of Americans have become suspicious of a medical model to explain sex offenders. Such offenders may plot and plan, scheme and stalk for months, utilize the most elaborate devices to avoid detection, even network with others and commercially profit from their foul acts.

But some psycho-apologist can always be found to claim the poor soul was deep in the grip of irresistible impulse when he was compelled to attack. Imagine the field day the expert-witness fraternity will have explaining how the castrated child molester who later killed his new victims was rendered insane as a result of the castration itself.

Sex offender treatment is the growth industry of the 1990s. Chemical castration already looms as a Get-Out-of-Jail-Free Card. Castration validates the sex offender's self-portrait: He is the victim; he can't help himself. It panders to our ugliest instincts, not the least of which is cowardice — the refusal to call evil by its name.

Nor can castration be defended because the perpetrator chooses it. Leaving aside the obvious issue of coercion, under what theory does a convicted criminal get to select his own (non-incarcerative) sentence?

America loves simple solutions to complex problems, especially solutions with political utility, like boot camp for youthful offenders. The last thing our cities need is muggers in better physical shape. When it comes to our own self-interest (and self-defense), the greatest sickness is stupidity. Castration qualifies . . . on all counts.

FOR MORE INFORMATION

The Association for the Treatment of Sexual Abusers, 10700 S.W. Beaverton-Hillsdale Highway, Suite 26, Beaverton, Ore. 97005-3035; (503) 643-1023. This nonprofit organization for professionals in the field of sex offender treatment is devoted to the development of professional standards and the dissemination of research.

CURE-SORT (Citizens United for the Rehabilitation of Errants — Sex Offenders Restored Through Treatment), P.O. Box 7782, Baltimore, Md. 21221-0782. CURE is a national organization founded by families of prisoners in 1972. This chapter, which represents sex offenders, lobbies for treatment of imprisoned sex offenders and alternatives to incarceration.

National Center for Missing and Exploited Children, 2101 Wilson Blvd., Suite 550, Arlington, Va. 22101-3052; (703) 235-3900. The center closely tracks state legislation affecting child abuse.

Safer Society Foundation, P.O. Box 340, Brandon, Vt. 05733-0340; (802) 247-3132. The foundation provides information on treating sexual abusers, conducts a nationwide survey every two years of treatment programs for sex offenders and provides a service that refers sex offenders to treatment.

National Center for Prosecution of Child Abuse, 99 Canal Center Plaza, Suite 510, Alexandria, Va. 22314; (703) 739-0321. The center tracks legislation and court cases related to sex offenders and assists prosecutors with their cases.

Continued from p. 55

returned to jail. Probation officers can also use intermediate steps like imposing a curfew.

Since May 1993, only 10 of the 800 sex offenders on probation in Maricopa County have committed new sex offenses, a recidivism rate of less than 1 percent, according to Scott. About 10 percent have committed technical violations like consorting with children.

Emphasis on Prevention

Increasingly, child abuse experts are urging more emphasis on improving prevention programs.

A recent report by the American Psychological Association says that traditional school programs that try to teach children to avoid sexually abusive situations "don't work very well," because children can't be expected to know what is, or isn't, appropriate touching in every situation. Instead, the report urges, programs should be expanded to target adult perpetrators.[27]

In Vermont, the Safer Society Foundation is pioneering a confidential telephone hotline called "Stop it Now!" to encourage molesters and potential offenders to seek treatment. Organizers also hope that offenders will turn themselves in to criminal authorities, noting that someone who does so is likely to receive more lenient treatment than someone arrested.

Other experts are working to root out sexual abusers even earlier. Since 1988, the C. Henry Kempe National Center for Prevention and Treatment of Child Abuse and Neglect in Denver, Colo., has been training teachers in 12 states to identify sexually abusive children. A curriculum developed by the center teaches educators to confront children about the behavior and to know when to refer them to counseling.

Gail Ryan, director of the center's Perpetration Prevention Project, says sexually abusive teens treated by the center often start their behavior in preschool and elementary school — with no adverse consequences from adults. "If we can interrupt the behavior and

get it back on a more normal course," she says, "that's the only way we'll slow the tide." ■

OUTLOOK

Legal Skirmishes

Activists on both sides of the sex-offender debate are looking to the Supreme Court for resolution of key issues. Yet even if the high court upholds state efforts to detain sex criminals beyond their sentence, the struggles in courtrooms and legislatures won't necessarily stop.

Klingensmith predicts further legal skirmishes as civil libertarians in some states charge that incarcerated sex offenders are not receiving meaningful counseling. "You can't just house them in what is really a prison — with a mental-hospital name," she says. "The court is still going to say, 'In application, that's punishment even though your law in spirit is constitutional.' "

If the Supreme Court strikes down sexual-predator laws as unconstitutional, state legislators are likely to crack down on sex offenders with harsher sentences.

According to Rutgers law Professor Brooks, the attacks on Washington state's sexual-predator statute already have fostered a get-tough attitude among many legislators. Brooks says the local sentiment is, "What we really ought to do is enact statutes like 'two strikes and you're in for life.' Forget treatment. Let's just punish these bastards." That approach would be "dreadful," in Brooks' view, because it would take in many sex offenders who could otherwise be successfully treated.

California has already moved in that direction. During the 1994 gubernatorial campaign, Republican Gov. Pete

Wilson signed a so-called "one-strike" bill. It calls for 25 years to life for a first-time sexual assault involving torture, mayhem, kidnaping or burglary with the intent to commit rape. [28]

During the campaign, Wilson also signed legislation to commit repeat sex offenders to secure mental health facilities before their scheduled release from prison. He emphasized that he saw the bill as a way to incapacitate sex criminals with mental disorders. "They'll only see the light of day when a jury is convinced they won't prey on innocent citizens," Wilson said. "For some, that should be a very long, long time."[29]

California's crackdown gained national attention recently when a notorious rapist was released from prison in December. Both of California's recently enacted sex offender laws had been signed too late to affect Reginald Muldrew.

Known as the "pillowcase rapist" because he put pillowcases over his victims' heads, Muldrew has been linked to 200 sex crimes in the Los Angeles area from 1976-78. In 1978, he was convicted of four rapes and 13 related sex, burglary and robbery offenses. He was sentenced to 25 years but eventually had nine years shaved off for good behavior.

"He is one of a handful of very high-profile cases where the Department of Corrections has no leeway to keep them in prison any longer than their prison sentence," says Christine May, a spokeswoman for the California Department of Corrections. Psychiatrists diagnosed Muldrew as having a mental disorder that still makes him dangerous, she said.

Three demonstrators from the Women's Coalition in Pasadena held pillowcases as they protested Muldrew's release from Vacaville State Prison on Dec. 5. Muldrew flew to Las Vegas and has not been heard from since, according to May.

Some of Washington state's older sex-crime prisoners also could go free

if the state's ground-breaking mental-commitment law is struck down. After the state passed the law in 1990, it enacted a "three strikes and you're out" law which sends criminals to prison for life after committing three serious offenses. In the future, many of the repeat sex offenders originally targeted by the 1990 mental-commitment law would be locked up for life under the three strikes law, according to Lieb at the Institute for Public Policy.

In fact, the debate over Washington's mental-commitment law could become moot if the Legislature passes a "one-strike" law covering most serious sex offenders, according to Berliner.

But Berliner cautions that such a law will take effect too late to apply to the 32 controversial sex offenders currently being held for mental-health therapy in Washington's prison system. If the sexual-predator law that put them there is declared unconstitutional by the Supreme Court, she says, "32 extremely dangerous people will be released all at once."   ■

Sarah Glazer is a Washington, D.C., writer who specializes in health and social-policy issues.

Notes

[1] For background, see "Violence Against Women," *The CQ Researcher*, Feb. 26, 1993, pp. 169-193.

[2] Donna D. Schram and Cheryl Darling Milloy, "Community Notification: A Study of Offender Characteristics and Recidivism," Washington State Institute for Public Policy, October 1995.

[3] Robert E. Freeman-Longo, "Public Notification of Sexual Offender Release: Prevention or Problem," Safer Society Foundation, 1995, p. 3.

[4] Schram and Milloy, *op. cit.*

[5] *Andre Brigham Young v. David Weston*, U.S. District Court, Western District of Washington at Seattle, Aug. 25, 1995.

[6] *Review of Sexual Predator Program*, Washington State Institute for Public Policy, February 1992, pp. 3-4 of appendix by Vernon L. Quinsey, Queens University, Ontario.

[7] See Lisa Grace Lednicer, "Linehan Confined Under New State Statute," *St. Paul Pioneer Press*,

July 28, 1995, p. 1A.

[8] See Judith V. Becker, "Offenders: Characteristics and Treatment," *The Future of Children*, summer/fall 1994, p. 181.

[9] *Ibid.*, p. 189.

[10] L. Furby, M. Weinrott and L. Blackshaw, "Sex Offender Recidivism: A Review," *Psychological Bulletin*, Vol. 105, No. 1, 1989, pp. 3-30.

[11] Gordon C. Nagayama Hall, "Sexual Offender Recidivism Revisited: A Meta-Analysis of Recent Treatment Studies," *Journal of Consulting and Clinical Psychology*, October 1995, pp. 802-809.

[12] Hanson presented his unpublished data in September 1995 to a conference in Cambridge, England, on sex offenders. It is based on 77 studies encompassing some 24,000 offenders in the U.S., Canada and Europe. Publication is scheduled in the May 1996 issue of *Forum on Corrections Research*, published by the Correctional Service of Canada.

[13] Allen J. Beck, "Recidivism of Prisoners Released in 1983," *Bureau of Justice Statistics Special Report*, April 1989, p. 6. This is the most recent year for which national recidivism rates are available.

[14] Becker, *op. cit.*, p. 183.

[15] See Jerome G. Miller, "Why the Scarlet 'A' Works Against Us," *Los Angeles Times*, Oct. 19, 1994, p. B7.

[16] Becker, *op. cit.*, p. 185.

[17] John Q. La Fond, "Washington's Sexually Violent Predator Law," *University of Puget Sound Law Review*, spring 1992, p. 661.

[18] *Ibid.*, pp. 668-69.

[19] The Children's Bureau is part of the Health and Human Services Department. For background, see "Child Sexual Abuse," *The CQ Researcher*, Jan. 15, 1993, pp. 25-48.

[20] Becker, *op. cit.*, p. 179.

[21] *Ibid.*

[22] *1994 Congressional Quarterly Almanac*, pp. 273-294. President Clinton signed the bill on Sept. 13, 1994.

[23] *Artway v. New Jersey*, Feb. 28, 1995.

[24] See Andre Henderson, "Corrections: The Scariest Criminal," Governing, Aug. 1, 1995, p. 34.

[25] *1994 Nationwide Survey of Treatment Programs and Models Serving Abuse-Reactive Children and Adolescent and Adult Sex Offenders*, Safer Society Foundation, 1994, p. 12.

[26] Becker, *op. cit.*, p. 192.

[27] American Psychological Association news release, "Psychologists Call for Overhaul of Child Protection System," Dec. 22, 1995, and "Psychological Issues Related to Child Maltreatment: Working Group Reports of the APA Coordinating Committee on Child Abuse and Neglect," *Journal of Clinical Child Psychology*, December 1995, p. 19.

[28]Amy Wallace and Eric Bailey, "'One Strike'

Bibliography

Selected Sources Used

Books

Allison, Dorothy, *Bastard Out of Carolina*, Plume, (paperback), 1993.
This novel, a National Book Award finalist in 1992, contains some unbearable descriptions of child abuse by an author who was abused herself as a child.

Vachss, Alice, *Sex Crimes*, Random House, 1993.
Former prosecutor Vachss tells the story of what it's like to prosecute sex offenders in New York.

Articles

Becker, Judith V., "Offenders: Characteristics and Treatment," *The Future of Children*, summer/fall 1994, pp. 176-197.
Becker, a professor of psychology and psychiatry at the University of Arizona, summarizes the research on treatments and causes of child molestation and concludes there's room for optimism.

Decter, Midge, "Megan's Law and *The New York Times*," *Commentary*, October 1994, p. 61.
Decter responds to criticisms of Megan's Law, arguing that, "Life imprisonment without parole for the sexual assaulter of a little girl is not only the one truly safe decision from the point of view of society; it might, ironically, be an act of kindness to the rapist as well."

Henderson, Andre, "Corrections: The Scariest Criminal," *Governing*, Aug. 1, 1995, p. 34.
A review of how states are responding to sex offenders and the constitutional cloud over the laws they are passing.

Kaihla, Paul, "Sex Offenders: Is there a Cure?" *MacLeans*, Feb. 13, 1995, pp. 56-57.
Kaihla quotes several prominent Canadian researchers in reviewing the debate over whether treatment reduces recidivism among sex offenders.

Popkin, James, et al., "Natural Born Predators," *U.S.*
News World Report, Sept. 19, 1994, p. 64.
Popkin looks at what communities have done to protect themselves against sex offenders.

McQuay, Larry Don, "The Case for Castration, Part I," *The Washington Monthly*, May 1994, p. 26.
Texas inmate McQuay, imprisoned for child molestation, argues that he should be castrated. "Without the right treatment, I believe that eventually I will rape, then murder my victims to keep them from reporting me," he writes. (See response to McQuay, below.)

Berlin, Fred S., "The Case for Castration, Part II," *The Washington Monthly*, May 1994, p. 28.
Psychiatrist Berlin responds that chemical castration, lowering testosterone through hormonal injections, is a better idea.

Wright, Lawrence, "A Rapist's Homecoming," *The New Yorker*, Sept. 4, 1995, pp. 56-69.
Wright describes the release of convicted rapist Donald Arthur Chapman from New Jersey's Avenel treatment facility for sex offenders. The warning of his therapist to county prosecutors that he was likely to commit another crime and the frightened response of his home town inspired the expansion of New Jersey's civil commitment statute under Megan's Law.

Reports and Studies

Cheryl Darling Milloy, "Community Notification: A Study of Offender Characteristics and Recidivism," Washington State Institute for Public Policy, October 1995.
This widely cited study found that community notification made little difference in sex offender recidivism.

"1994 Nationwide Survey of Treatment Programs and Models Servicing Abuse-Reactive Children and Adolescents and Adult Sex Offenders," Safe Society Foundation, 1994.
This nationwide survey is conducted every two years by the Brandon, Vt., based foundation.

The Sex Offender Down the Street;
In Texas City, Signs Send Warning—and Stir Debate

Paul Duggan

CORPUS CHRISTI, Tex.—The yard sign, two feet wide and 18 inches high, is posted on a patch of grass near the door of James Williams's first-floor apartment. "DANGER," it warns, in bold white letters across a background of red. "Registered Sex Offender Lives Here."

The placard, which Williams, 43, calls "humiliating," has been drawing stares for more than a week, since state Judge J. Manuel Banales of Corpus Christi ordered it put up.

Banales placed Williams on probation in 1999 for sexually groping his then-girlfriend's 15-year-old daughter. But Williams is far from alone in his embarrassment. In a judicial initiative that defense lawyers here describe as highly unusual, if not unique, Banales ordered identical signs posted at the homes of 13 other first-time sex offenders who are on probation in this Gulf Coast city.

"It's a return to the days of the scarlet letter," complained Gerald Rogen, president of the Coastal Bend Criminal Defense Lawyers Association, who said he plans a legal challenge to Banales's action. "It's nothing less than public branding."

In an interview, Banales said he was confident his decision would stand. "This is a matter of public safety," said the judge, a Democrat and former criminal defense lawyer serving his fourth four-year term on the bench. "I have a responsibility to protect the community."

In ordering the probationers to post the signs and identify themselves in other ways, including with bumper stickers, Banales has stirred a local debate that reflects a nearly decade-old, nationwide disagreement between advocates for victims and civil libertarians.

In the 1990s, Congress and state legislatures passed laws aimed at increasing community awareness of sex offenders' names and addresses. But at what point do these public safety efforts begin intruding on privacy rights? At what point do the measures cease to be reasonable and become punitive?

"Between protecting the safety of children and protecting the rights of a person on probation for a sex offense, the balance has to tilt toward the children," Banales said.

Some of the 14 offenders here have been on probation for months, others for years. None was imprisoned. Under Texas's sex-offender registration and community notification laws, their names, addresses, photos and criminal records have been advertised in local newspapers and are available on a state Web site. But Banales said he recently decided that ads and Web postings aren't always enough.

After reviewing the records of all sex offenders who were placed on probation in his court in the last decade and who remain under supervision, Banales summoned 54 of them to a hearing on May 18, according to probation officials. They said about 42 of the offenders showed up.

Banales toughened the probation conditions for many of them and ordered placards in 14 cases. The judge said he realized the signs could incite vigilante violence, but decided that "warning and protecting our children" had to take precedence.

And he ordered more than just yard signs. Like the other 13 men deemed by Banales to be "potential risks for reoffending," Williams received a court-issued bumper sticker for his car: "DANGER. Registered Sex Offender In Vehicle." Lest any of the probationers escape public notice by traveling in someone else's car, the judge gave each a small, plastic placard with a suction cup attached—similar to a "Baby on Board" sign, but bearing the same blunt message as the bumper sticker.

Like the others, Williams, a divorced aircraft mechanic who lives by himself, was ordered to affix the suction-cup sign to the rear window of any private vehicle he rides in.

From the *Washington Post*, May 29, 2001. Reprinted with Permission.

"I feel like a hermit," said Williams, who has rarely ventured from his apartment since "the shock" of Banales's order. He said he was too embarrassed to go to work and has left home only to buy food and visit his probation officer.

"I've tried very hard to get my life together" in the last 28 months, since being placed on four years of probation, he said. "I've done everything they told me to do," including performing community service, undergoing counseling and submitting to polygraph tests.

On the polygraph tests, Williams said, some of his responses to questions concerning his sexual behavior while on probation have been judged "deceptive," although he said his answers were true. "I have never done anything wrong" in 28 months, Williams said. "I just can't pass the damn test." He said Banales cited the poor polygraph findings in issuing his order.

"I know people are out there driving by, looking at me like I'm the lowest thing on the Earth," Williams said. "They're thinking I'm some kind of rapist, hurting little children."

John Lee, 34, an insulation installer, also admitted to sexually groping the 15-year-old daughter of an acquaintance. Banales put him on probation for five years in March 2000.

Since then, Lee said, "I've been walking a straight and narrow line," except for a night several months ago when he drank beer with his father. Because his unforced sexual encounter with the teenager occurred while he was drunk, Lee said, he is required to stay alcohol-free during his probation.

He owned up to the drinking violation during a counseling session and a polygraph test, he said, and the admission came back to haunt him at the May 18 hearing before Banales.

Lee said he was "scared and sick" after the hearing as he returned to the apartment he shares with his father, carrying his sign, sticker and suction-cup placard. "They're making it out like I broke into someone's house and put a gun to their head and raped them and killed them," he said.

He fastened the sign to the apartment door instead of posting it outside, he said. That night, Lee's father said, he answered a loud knock and had an ugly confrontation with a stranger who was irate about "perverts living in the neighborhood." The father said he closed the door when the man began to threaten violence. The next morning, he said, the sign was missing.

As for the bumper sticker, Lee said that shortly after he put it on his pickup truck, he was harassed at a traffic light by a group of men in a car. He said one of them pointed a finger at him as if it were a gun, and squeezed an imaginary trigger. "I pulled over and took the sticker off," Lee said. "I have to decide what's more important, staying alive or that damn bumper sticker. And I choose my life."

More than a few of the offenders summoned to court by Banales on May 18 are on probation for offenses similar to Williams's and Lee's. In other cases, the victims were much younger.

But "these weren't people who drove around the streets in vans abducting kids and sexually assaulting them. If that was the case, they'd be in prison," said Fate Mays, a senior probation official here. "Some of them were 18- or 20-year-old adults who had sex with their 15- or 16-year-old girlfriends."

The Nueces County probation department in Corpus Christi supervises about 225 sex offenders who have appeared before eight judges in the county, including the 54 probationers from Banales's court. "I don't think the other judges intend to [order signs] just yet," Mays said. "They're taking a wait-and-see attitude."

But Mays said he strongly supports the signs, citing two disturbing cases here in the past year involving repeat sex offenders who preyed on children.

One involved Jaime Guerra, 39, who had been convicted of sexually abusing a child in the early 1990s. Last August, authorities said, Guerra tried to rape a 12-year-old girl after luring her into his home with a pet rabbit. The girl told police that she was able to fight him off. Guerra was convicted of aggravated kidnapping on May 10 and sentenced to life in prison.

Banales said Guerra's case and a similar one in Corpus Christi inspired him to review the files of offenders he had placed on probation over the years and toughen restrictions. Probation officials helped decide which offenders would get signs.

continues

"If there had been a sign up" at Guerra's house, Mays said, "the parents of that 12-year-old girl could have told her: 'When you're walking to school, walk on the other side of the street. Don't go near that house.'"

Requiring sex offenders to register with local police is a concept that dates back a half-century in the United States. But laws dealing with community notification—by newspaper ads, mailings, door-to-door police visits and other means—are relatively new. Since 1990, every state and the federal government have enacted such statutes, commonly called "Megan's laws"—named for a 7-year-old New Jersey girl who was raped and strangled by a twice-convicted sex offender living in her neighborhood.

In legal and legislative fights over the scope of notification, victims' advocates have generally prevailed over civil libertarians. Activists on both sides of that debate said they could not recall previous instances of judges ordering wholesale postings of yard signs. Activists said signs have usually been reserved for extraordinary, individual cases.

Rogen, of the defense lawyers association, said he plans to argue that Banales exceeded the bounds of Texas law. But the judge said the law gives him discretion to act as he did.

"A person might kill once, or a person might rob a bank once, but sex offenders have a propensity to commit similar offenses again and again," Banales said. "That's what worries me."

Simmons-Harris v. Zelman

The case of *Simmons-Harris v. Zelman*, 234 F.3d 945 (2000) was decided by the United States Court of Appeals for the 6th Circuit in December 2000. Participants in the simulation will study this particular court case and attempt to persuade the Supreme Court either to grant or deny certiorari. If granted certiorari, the case will be argued before the Court, and the Court will hand down a ruling. Participants should read the entire case to familiarize themselves with the legal reasoning employed and to understand how the lower court decided it.

Simmons-Harris v. Zelman
Nos. 00–3055/3060/3063
United States Court of Appeals for the Sixth Circuit
Filed: December 11, 2000

On appeal from the United States District Court for the Northern District of Ohio at Cleveland. Nos. 99–01740, 99–01818—Solomon Oliver, Jr., District Judge.

JUDGES: Before: RYAN, SILER, and CLAY, Circuit Judges.

JUSTICE CLAY delivered the opinion of the court, in which JUSTICE SILER joined. JUSTICE RYAN delivered a separate opinion concurring in part and dissenting in part.

OPINION OF THE COURT

CLAY, Circuit Judge.

Defendants and Intervenors Dr. Susan Tave Zelman, et al.; Senel Taylor, et al.; and Hanna Perkins School, et al., appeal from the order entered by the United States District Court for the Northern District of Ohio, enjoining on summary judgment the Ohio Pilot Project Scholarship Program on the ground that it violates the Establishment Clause of the First Amendment. For the following reasons, we AFFIRM.

I

In 1995, Ohio's General Assembly adopted the Ohio Pilot Project Scholarship Program ("voucher program" or "the program") in response to an order by the United States District Court that placed the Cleveland School District under the direct management and supervision of the State Superintendent of Public Instruction due to mismanagement by the local school board. The voucher program covers any state school district that has been the subject of a federal court order "requiring supervision and operational management of the district by the state superintendent." Ohio Rev. Code §3313.975(A). The program provides scholarships to children residing within the applicable district in grades kindergarten through eighth grade. See Ohio Rev. Code §3313.975(C)(1). The program gives "preference to students from low-income families," defining them as those whose families' income is less than 200% of the poverty line. See Ohio Rev. Code §3313.978(A). "Scholarships may be awarded to students who are not from low-income families only if all students from low-income families have been given first consideration for placement." Cleveland Scholarship and Tutoring Program, Administration Procedures Manual, 1-11 (J.A. at 1358) (emphasis original). Over sixty percent of the children receiving scholarships in the program are from families with incomes at or below the poverty line.

The voucher program pays scholarships according to family income. The program requires participating private schools to cap tuition at $2500 per student per year and pays 90% of whatever tuition the school actually charges for low-income families; for other families, the State pays 75% of the school's tuition up to a maximum of $1875. See Ohio Rev. Code. §§3313.976(A)(8), 3313.978(A). Each scholarship for children attending a private school is payable to the parents of the student entitled to the scholarship. Ohio Rev. Code §3313.979. Scholarship checks are mailed to the school selected by the parents, where the parents are required to endorse the checks over to the school in order to pay tuition.

Schools wishing to be designated as program participants eligible to enroll scholarship students must register with the voucher program. Private schools located within the boundaries of the Cleveland school district which meet the State's educational standards may participate. See Ohio Rev. Code §3313.976(A)(1) and (3). Schools are required to follow the program's priority rules regarding the placement of students and may not discriminate on the basis of race, religion, or ethnic background; advocate or foster unlawful behavior; or teach hatred of any person or group on the basis of race, ethnicity, national origin, or religion. See Ohio Rev. Code §3313.976(A)(6). Public schools in districts adjacent to the district in which the voucher program is implemented may also register for the program and "receive scholarship payments on behalf of parents," but none of the public schools in districts adjacent to Cleveland have done so. Ohio Rev. Code §3313.976(C). The checks for program participants at public schools are made out to the participating school district rather than to the parents. No public schools have registered for the program since its enactment.

For the 1999–2000 school year, 3,761 students enrolled in the program; 60% of the enrollees are from families at or below the poverty level. Of these, 3,632 (96%) are enrolled in sectarian schools. At one time in the course of the program, as many as 22% of the students enrolled in the program attended nonreligious schools. During the 1999–2000 school year, fifty-six schools registered to participate in the program; forty-six (82%) are church-affiliated. Program monies may be used by the participating schools for whatever purpose they deem appropriate; the voucher program does not place restrictions on the use of funds made available under the program.

The sectarian schools vary in their religious affiliation and approaches; however, the handbooks and mission statements of these schools reflect that most believe in interweaving religious beliefs with secular subjects. The sectarian schools also follow religious guidelines, including instruction in religion and mandated participation in religious services; interweaving of Christian doctrines with science and language arts classes; requiring that "all learning take place in an atmosphere of religious ideals," St. Vincent de Paul School, Parent Handbook 11 (1999–2000); and designing educational scholarship in order "to make . . . faith become living, conscious, and active through the light of instruction . . . religious truths and values permeate the whole atmosphere of the school." Saint Rocco School, Parent-Student Handbook 1 (1999–2000). Other sectarian schools in the voucher program believe that "the one cardinal objective of education to which all others point is to develop devotion to God as our Creator, Redeemer, and Sanctifier," Saint John Nottingham Lutheran School, Parent Handbook 2 (1999–2000); and to require students to "pledge allegiance to the Christian flag and to the Savior for whose Kingdom it stands, One Savior crucified, risen and coming again with life and liberty for all who believe." Calvary Center Academy, Parent-Student Handbook 24 (1999–2000).

In prior litigation, Doris Simmons-Harris, one of the Plaintiffs herein, brought a state court lawsuit challenging the constitutionality of the voucher program under multiple provisions of the Ohio Constitution, and under the Establishment Clause of the United States Constitution. On May 27, 1999, the Ohio Supreme Court issued a judgment in favor of Plaintiffs, holding that the 1995 voucher program had been enacted in violation of the one-subject rule of the Ohio Constitution, and "must be stricken" from the Ohio statute books. See *Simmons-Harris v. Goff,*

711 N.E.2d 203, 216 (Ohio 1999). However, a majority of the justices rejected Plaintiffs' claims that the program violated the Establishment Clause. Id. at 207–11, 218–19. Those justices reasoned that "[t]he Nyquist holding [had been] undermined" by subsequent cases and was thus no longer good law. Id. at 208. A concurring opinion noted that "[w]ith regard to the rest of the majority opinion [the section not dealing with the one-subject rule], . . . I find a number of the other assertions by the majority to be advisory in nature." Id. at 216 (Douglas, J., joined by Resnick and Sweeney, JJ., concurring in the judgment only). Since this case, the Ohio Legislature has re-enacted the voucher program in a manner remedying the one-subject problem; however, the 1999 program is in all relevant aspects, the same as the original pilot scholarship program enacted by the Legislature in 1995.

On July 20, 1999, Simmons-Harris, the parent of a minor child enrolled in the Cleveland City School District for the 1999–2000 school year; Marla Franklin, a teacher in the Lorain City School District; and Steven Behr, pastor of Our Savior/Nuestro Salvado Church in Lorain, Ohio, filed suit in Case No. 1:99cv1740, against Defendant Dr. Susan Tave Zelman in her official capacity as Superintendent of Public Instruction for the Ohio Department of Education, seeking to enjoin a portion of the program on the ground that it violated the Establishment Clause of the First Amendment. On July 29, 1999, Sue Gatton, chair of Citizens Against Vouchers; Mary Murphy, a teacher in the Cleveland City School District; Michael Debose, a pastor in Cuyahoga County, Ohio; Cheryl Debose and Glenn Altschuld, Ohio Taxpayers; and Deidra Pearson, the parent of a child enrolled in the Cleveland City School District, filed suit in Case No. 1:99cv1818 against Defendants Dr. Susan Tave Zelman, in her official capacity as Superintendent; the State of Ohio through its General Assembly, Governor and other agents; and Saundra Berry, in her official capacity as Program Administrator of the Ohio Pilot Scholarship Program, seeking the same injunctive relief as in Case No. 1:99cv1740.

Proposed Intervenors Senel Taylor, Johnnietta McGrady, Christine Suma, Arkela Winston, and Amy Hudock, on their own behalf and as natural guardians of their respective children, filed an answer to Simmons-Harris' complaint on July 27, 1999. Proposed Intervenors Hanna Perkins School, Ivy Chambers, Carol Lambert, Our Lady of Peace School, Westpark Lutheran School Association, Inc., Lutheran Memorial Association of Cleveland, and Delores Jones, filed an answer to Simmons-Harris' complaint on August 2, 1999.

On August 13, 1999, the district court held a preliminary injunction hearing in both cases, and on August 24, 1999, granted Plaintiffs the injunctive relief sought. In the same order, the district court consolidated the two cases, and found that the Ohio Supreme Court's decision in *Simmons v. Goff*, 711 N.E.2d 203 (Ohio 1999), did not preclude federal consideration of the constitutional challenge to the voucher program because the Ohio court's decision rested on a state ground which independently supported its resolution of the case. Thereafter, on August 27, 1999, the district court granted in part Defendants' motion for a stay of the preliminary injunction.

On August 24, 1999, the same day that the district court granted Plaintiffs' motion for a preliminary injunction, the State and the two intervening Defendants appealed that decision to this Court. After the district court's August 27, 1999, order granting a limited stay of its preliminary injunction, all Defendants filed revised briefs with this Court, appealing the preliminary injunction with regard to students who were new to the voucher program—i.e., the portion of the preliminary injunction not stayed by the district court's August 27, 1999 order. While those appeals were pending, the State filed a motion for a stay of the preliminary injunction with the United

States Supreme Court, which the Supreme Court granted by a vote of 5–4 on November 5, 1999, pending this Court's final disposition of the entire appeal. See *Simmons-Harris v. Zelman*, 120 S. Ct. 443 (1999). Thereafter, this Court entered an order on November 15, 1999, concluding that the Supreme Court's decision granting the State's motion for a stay rendered moot Defendants' pending motions for a stay in this Court. The case proceeded in the district court on an expedited basis.

On October 15, 1999, all parties stipulated that the handbooks, mission statements and brochures of the schools participating in the Cleveland scholarship program are "authentic, speak for themselves, have been made available to the parents of the scholarship students and are not false or misleading. Some of these documents however may not accurately reflect admission standards that had to be revised." Plaintiffs and Defendants both filed motions for summary judgment on November 1, 1999.

On November 29, 1999, the district court denied Intervenor Taylor's motion to have the following question certified to the Ohio Supreme Court: "Does Ohio law give preclusive effect to the resolution of the Establishment Clause claim in *Simmons-Harris v. Goff*, 711 N.E.2d 203 (Ohio 1999)?"

The district court granted Plaintiffs' motion for summary judgment on December 20, 1999, finding that the voucher program violated the Establishment Clause; enjoined Defendants from administering the program; and denied Defendants' motion for summary judgment. See *Simmons-Harris v. Zelman*, 72 F. Supp. 2d 834, 836 (N.D. Ohio 1999). The court stayed its summary judgment order with Plaintiffs' consent pending review by this Court. Defendants and Intervenors appealed to this Court on January 12, 2000.

II

We recognize the significance that this issue holds for many members of our society. The issue of school vouchers has been the subject of intense political and public commentary, discussion, and attention in recent years, and we would be remiss if we failed to acknowledge the seriousness of the concerns this case has raised. We do not, however, have the luxury of responding to advents in educational policy with academic discourse on practical solutions to the problem of failing schools; nor may we entertain a discussion on what might be legally acceptable in a hypothetical school district. We may only apply the controlling law to the case and statute before us.

The courts do not make educational policy; we do not sit in omnipotent judgment as to the efficacy of one scheme or program versus another. The design or specifics of a program intended to remedy the problem of failing schools and to rectify educational inequality must be reserved to the states and the school boards within them, with one caveat: the proposed program may not run afoul of the freedoms guaranteed to all citizens in the Constitution. In other words, the determinations of states and school boards cannot infringe upon the necessary separation between church and state. We therefore consider the program presented before us under the controlling precedents of the United States Supreme Court and this Court to determine whether such infringement has occurred.

This Court reviews the district court's grant of summary judgment de novo. See *Coles v. Cleveland Bd. of Educ.*, 171 F.3d 369, 376 (6th Cir. 1999). Summary judgment is proper when "the pleadings, depositions, answers to interrogatories, and admissions on file, together with the affidavits, if any, show that there is no genuine issue as to any material fact and that the moving party is entitled to judgment as a matter of law." Fed. R. Civ. P. 56(c). There is no genuine issue of material fact when the "record taken as a whole could not lead a rational trier of fact to find for the nonmoving party." *Matsushita Elec. Indus. Co. v. Zenith Radio Corp.*, 475 U.S. 574, 587 (1986).

The Establishment Clause provides that "Congress shall make no law respecting an establishment of religion. . . ." U.S. Const., amend. I. In *Lemon v. Kurtzman*, 403 U.S. 602, 612–13 (1971), the Supreme Court set forth the following test to determine whether a statute passes muster under the Establishment Clause: 1) the statute must have a secular legislative purpose; 2) the principal or primary effect of the statute must be one that neither advances nor inhibits religion; and 3) the statute must not foster excessive entanglement with religion. If a statute fails any portion of this test, it violates the Establishment Clause. Id. The Supreme Court has applied the Lemon test regularly in the context of schools and education. See, e.g., *Kiryas Joel Sch. Dist. v. Gromet*, 512 U.S. 687 (1994) (drawing a separate school district for one religion violates the Establishment Clause); *Stone v. Graham*, 449 U.S. 39 (1989)(posting Ten Commandments on walls of public school violates Establishment Clause); *Bowen v. Kendrick*, 487 U.S. 589 (1988) (holding that Establishment Clause does not prevent religious organizations from participating in federally funded program); *Edwards v. Aguillard*, 482 U.S. 578 (1987) (overturning statute which required the teaching of Creationism in public schools); *Aguilar v. Felton*, 473 U.S. 402 (1985) (paying public school employees to teach in parochial school violates the Establishment Clause), overruled by *Agostini v. Felton*, 521 U.S. 203 (1997); *Grand Rapids Sch. Dist. v. Ball*, 473 U.S. 373 (1985) (finding a shared time program to be a violation of Establishment Clause), overruled by *Agostini v. Felton*, 521 U.S. 203 (1997); *Mueller v. Allen*, 463 U.S. 388 (1983)(permitting taxpayers to deduct from state income tax expenses incurred in sending children to parochial schools does not violate Establishment Clause); *Roemer v. Bd. of Pub. Works*, 426 U.S. 736 (1976)(finding no violation of Establishment Clause in providing government aid to both public and private universities).

The Supreme Court and individual justices have introduced variations on the Lemon test in other contexts. See *Lee v. Weisman*, 505 U.S. 577, 592–98 (1992) (using coercion test developed by Justice Kennedy to hold that school could not provide for nonsectarian prayer to be given at graduation by school-selected clergyman); *County of Alleghany v. ACLU*, 492 U.S. 573, 594–602, 655–79 (1989) (using two-part test developed by Justice O'Connor—Establishment Clause is violated when 1) government is excessively entangled with religion, or 2) government endorses or disapproves of religion—as part of the Lemon test regarding government displays of objects with religious connotations; introducing Justice Kennedy's two-part coercion test—1) government may not coerce participation in religion, and 2) government may not directly benefit religion—in his concurrence); *Wallace v. Jaffree*, 472 U.S. 38, 56 & n.42 (1985) (using Justice O'Connor's two-part test as part of the Lemon analysis and finding it appropriate to determine whether the government's purpose is to endorse or disapprove of religion); *Lynch v. Donnelly*, 465 U.S. 668, 687–94 (1984) (introducing Justice O'Connor's two-part test).

In *Agostini v. Felton*, 521 U.S. 203 (1997), the Court reaffirmed the importance of the Lemon test in Establishment Clause cases involving school aid, but noted that the entanglement prong could be considered as an aspect of the effects inquiry. Agostini found "three primary criteria" used by the Court in evaluating whether government aid has the effect of advancing religion: whether the statute or programs in question "result in governmental indoctrination; define its recipients by reference to religion; or create an excessive entanglement." Id. at 234.

The Supreme Court has not overturned or rescinded the Lemon test even as it has used its framework to shape differing analyses. Although in Agostini, the Court articulated the primary criteria it would utilize to determine whether a government-aid program impermissibly advanced or endorsed religion, the Court has not necessarily limited itself to considering solely those criteria. Rather, it seems evident that the Agostini Court illustrated the Lemon test's flexibility and its evolution from the relatively rigid three-part test to an approach in which the varying components of a particular program or statute are analyzed with regard to their impact on, in the context of schools, the relevant students or communities. We therefore look to these components as aspects of the proper analysis under Lemon, but acknowledge that precedent does not limit itself to only these components should other components previously utilized by the Court be relevant, such as coercion of citizens, endorsement of religion, and direct benefit to religion. See *Mitchell v. Helms*, 120 S. Ct 2530, 2556 (2000) (O'Connor, J., concurring) (finding that Agostini represents a general framework for approaching questions concerning neutral school-aid programs but recognizing that these type of cases depend on the particular facts of each case).

Of the cases which follow Lemon, we find the most persuasive, in that it is on point with the matter at hand, to be *Committee for Public Education v. Nyquist*, 413 U.S. 756 (1973). In Nyquist, a New York State statute established, among other aid, a tuition grant program which provided for partial tuition reimbursement to low-income parents whose children attended private elementary or secondary schools. See id. at 761–70. The tuition reimbursement plan applied to parents of children who attended any private school, not solely sectarian schools, and was limited to 50% of tuition paid. Id. at 764. At the time the plan was challenged, nearly 20% of New York's school-age children attended nonpublic schools, and approximately 85% of these schools were sectarian. Id. at 768. The Nyquist Court noted that although "the characteristics of individual schools may vary widely from [the] profile," institutions which qualified for assistance under the statute were ones that included religious instruction and requirements as part of their academic curriculum. See id. at 767–68.

Following Lemon, the Nyquist Court found that the New York statute passed the first prong of the Lemon test—whether the statute had a secular purpose—because the tuition reimbursement program promoted pluralism and diversity among New York's public and private schools, and alleviated concern that the State's overburdened public schools would be harmed if a large number of children who had previously been attending private schools decided to return to the public schools. See 413 U.S. at 773. The Court did "not question the propriety, and fully secular content, of New York's interest in preserving a healthy and safe educational environment for all of its schoolchildren." Id.

Under the second prong of the Lemon test—that the statute neither advance nor inhibit religion—the New York statute did not fare as well. The Court next found that the New York reimbursement program failed because "[i]n the absence of an effective means of guaranteeing that the state aid derived from public funds will be used exclusively for secular, neutral, and non-ideological purposes, it is clear from our cases that direct aid in whatever form is invalid." 413 U.S. at 780. The Court opined that the fact that program grants were delivered to parents rather than schools was "only one among many factors to be considered." Id. at 781. The Court rested its analysis on the premise that there had been " 'no endeavor to guarantee the separation between secular and religious educational functions and to ensure the State financial aid supports only the former.' " Id. at 783 (quoting Lemon, 403 U.S. at 613). "By reimbursing parents for a portion of their tuition bill, the State seeks to relieve their financial burdens sufficiently to assure that they continue to have the option to send their children to religion-oriented schools." Id. The Court noted that "while the other purposes for that aid—to perpetuate a pluralistic educational environment and to protect the fiscal integrity of overburdened public schools—are certainly unexceptionable, the effect of the aid is unmistakably to provide desired financial support for nonpublic, sectarian institutions." Id.

The Nyquist Court also recognized and discarded the state's arguments that it was of controlling significance that New York's program called for reimbursement of tuition already paid, thus ensuring that the parent is free to spend that tuition money in any manner he or she sees fit. 413 U.S. at 785–86. "[I]f the grants are offered as an incentive to parents to send their children to sectarian schools by making unrestricted cash payments to them, the Establishment Clause is violated. . . . Whether the grant is labeled a reimbursement, a reward, or a subsidy, its substantive impact is still the same." Id. at 786. The Court also rejected the state's argument that the plan paid for only a portion of the tuition at a sectarian school, saying "if accepted, this argument would provide the foundation for massive, direct subsidization of sectarian elementary and secondary schools." Id. at 787.

The cases of *Everson v. Board of Education,* 330 U.S. 1 (1947), and *Board of Education v. Allen,* 392 U.S. 236 (1968) were carefully distinguished by the Court. In Everson, the Court upheld tax deductions for parents who expended bus fare for children who attended religious schools, reasoning that the bus fare program was analogous to the provision of services such as police and fire protection, sewage disposal, highways and sidewalks for parochial schools. See 330 U.S. at 17–18. The Court found that these services, common to all citizens, are "so separate and so indisputably marked off from the religious function, that they may fairly be viewed as reflections of a neutral posture toward religious institutions." Id. at 18. In Allen, the Court upheld a statute which allowed secular textbooks to be provided to children attending religious schools, finding that "the State claims no right to distribute religious literature," and noting that "we cannot assume that school authorities . . . are unable to distinguish between secular and religious books." 392 U.S. at 244–45. The Nyquist Court distinguished these two cases not only based on their neutral posture toward religion, but on the fact that in both of those cases, "the class of beneficiaries included all schoolchildren, those in public as well as those in private schools." 413 U.S. at 782 n.38, (citing *Tilton v. Richardson,* 403 U.S. 672 (1970) (making federal aid available to all institutions of higher learning)).

The Court noted that unlike in Everson and Allen, the tuition grants in Nyquist were not a neutral attempt to provide comparable benefits to all parents of schoolchildren whether enrolled in public or nonpublic schools, as the "grants to parents of private schoolchildren are given in addition to the right that they have to send their children to public schools totally at state expense." 413 U.S. at 782 n.38 (internal quotation marks omitted). The Court additionally determined that this argument of neutrality, if upheld, would be overly broad, providing "a basis for approving through tuition grants the complete subsidization of all religious schools on the ground that such action is necessary if the State is fully to equalize the position of parents who elect such schools—a result wholly at variance with the Establishment Clause." Id.

The Supreme Court has revisited many of the issues raised in Nyquist. In *Agostini v. Felton,* 521 U.S. 203, 237 (1997), the Court stated that "[w]e do not acknowledge, and we do not hold, that other courts should conclude our more recent cases have, by implication, overruled an earlier precedent." The Court continued to reaffirm "that if a precedent of this Court has direct application in a case, yet appears to rest on reasons rejected in some other line of decisions, **the Court of Appeals should follow the case which directly controls,** leaving to this Court the prerogative of overruling its own decisions." Id. (emphasis added). The Supreme Court has refrained from overruling Nyquist, and has instead distinguished various cases on the basis of their facts; this Court has accordingly followed that approach. "A single factual difference consequently can serve to entangle or free a particular governmental practice from the reach of the [Establishment] Clause's constitutional prohibition." Coles, 171 F.3d at 376. We therefore look to relevant case law to assist us by analogy in analyzing the factual discrepancies between this case and Nyquist.

In *Mueller v. Allen,* 463 U.S. 388 (1983), the Court found constitutional a Minnesota statute which allowed state taxpayers to deduct on their state income tax certain tuition, transportation and educational expenses of their children attending elementary or secondary schools. Following the Lemon test, the Court agreed that the statute had the secular purpose of defraying the cost of education for all parents, regardless of the type of school their children attend. Id. at 395. Analyzing the effect of the statute, the Court held that the program did not have a primary effect of advancing religion because the tax deduction was a traditional area for state legislatures to codify policies which "achieve an equitable distribution of the tax burden," and because the deduction was available for educational expenses incurred by all parents, whether their children attended public schools, nonsectarian private schools, or church-affiliated schools. Id. at 396–98.

The Court found it compelling that the deduction was available for all parents with school age children, stating that this aspect was "vitally different from the scheme struck down in Nyquist. There, public assistance amounting to tuition grants was provided only to parents of children in nonpublic schools." Id. at 398. The Court analogized the tax deduction scheme as similar to the G.I. Bill, or other forms of "public assistance made available generally without regard to the sectarian–nonsectarian, or public–nonpublic nature of the institution benefitted." Id. The Court found it significant that under the Minnesota plan, governmental aid was only channeled through the parents, rather than directly paid to the parochial institutions, and noted that it would not base the constitutionality of a statute on the consideration of yearly statistical evidence concerning which nonsectarian schools—religious or otherwise—benefitted from the tax deduction. Id. at 401. The Court stated that the Establishment Clause is not a bar to "the sort of attenuated financial benefit, ultimately controlled by the private choices of individual parents, that eventually flows to parochial schools from the neutrally available tax benefit at issue in this case." Id. at 400.

In *Witters v. Washington Department of Services for the Blind,* 474 U.S. 481 (1986), the Supreme Court found constitutional a Washington State program which provided vocational rehabilitation assistance grants to a blind individual who attended a Christian college in the hope of becoming a pastor. The Court found the statute's purpose "unmistakably secular," id. at 486, and found that unlike Nyquist, "any aid provided under Washington's program that ultimately flows to religious institutions does so only as a result of the genuinely independent and private choices of aid recipients." Id. at 488. The fact that the vocational assistance was paid directly to the student, who could expend the educational funds on "wholly secular education," persuaded the Court to find that the program did not create an incentive to apply the aid to religious education. Id. "Aid recipients' choices are made among a huge variety of possible careers, of which only a small handful are sectarian. . . . Nothing in the record indicates that . . . any significant portion of the aid expended under the Washington program as a whole will end up flowing to religious education." Id. The Court also found that "the mere circumstance that petitioner has chosen to use neutrally available state aid to help pay for his religious education [does not] confer any message of state endorsement of religion." Id. at 489.

In *Agostini v. Felton,* the Court held that the Establishment Clause did not bar a New York program which sent public school teachers into parochial schools to provide remedial education to disadvantaged children. Recognizing that there had been significant changes in Establishment Clause jurisprudence, the Court found that it could no longer presume "that the placement of public employees on parochial school grounds inevitably results in the impermissible effect of state-sponsored indoctrination or constitutes a symbolic union between government and religion." 521 U.S. at 223. The Court noted that those direct aid programs where grants are "made available generally without regard to the sectarian–nonsectarian, or public–nonpublic nature of the institution benefitted [are valid departures from the general rule] that all government aid that directly aids the educational function of religious schools is invalid." Id. at 225. Relying on an earlier case which had found it permissible to place a public school sign language interpreter into a private parochial school under the Individuals with Disabilities Education Act, 20 U.S.C. §1400, the Court determined that these instances involve situations where money ultimately goes to religious schools "only as a result of the genuinely independent and private choices of individuals." Id. at 225–26 (citing *Zobrest v. Catalina Foothills Sch. Dist.,* 509 U.S. 1 (1993)). The Court noted as a central part of its analysis that the services provided by public school employees were remedial, stating that the "services do not, therefore, reliev[e] sectarian schools of costs they otherwise would have borne in educating their students." Id. at 228. The Court concluded that the New York program services "are available to all children who meet the Act's eligibility requirements, no matter what their religious beliefs or where they go to school." Id. at 232.

The Supreme Court revisited this issue this past term. By a plurality, the Court upheld a program to loan educational materials and equipment to private religious schools which channeled federal funds through state agencies. See *Mitchell v. Helms,* 120 S. Ct. 2530 (2000). Writing for four justices, Justice Thomas concluded that the critical question in cases of government aid to religious schools is whether the government aid is neutral: whether it results from the genuinely independent and private choices of individual parents. See id. at 2541–44. Justice Thomas noted that the nexus between neutrality and private choice was the prominent, even the chief factor, in upholding government aid in Agostini, Zobrest, Witters, and Mueller, and found that there is a close relationship between private choice and the question of whether a program creates a financial incentive to undertake religious schooling. See id. at 2543.

The opinion goes on to state that "[i]f aid to schools, even direct aid, is neutrally available and, before reaching or benefitting any religious school, first passes through the hands (literally or figuratively) of numerous private citizens who are free to direct the aid elsewhere, the government has not provided any support of religion." 120 S. Ct. at 2544 (internal citations omitted). The opinion recognizes that there exist "special Establishment Clause dangers when money is given to religious schools or entities directly rather than, as in Witters and Mueller, indirectly." Id. at 2546 (internal citations omitted). In a footnote, Justice Thomas hypothesized "that the principles of neutrality and private choice would be adequate to address those special risks." Id. at 2547 n.8. He continued to find that at least in regards to Nyquist, the prohibition against direct payments was linked to "serious concerns about whether the payments were truly neutral." Id.

Although Justice O'Connor concurred in the judgment, she wrote separately in Mitchell based upon her belief that "the plurality announces a rule of unprecedented breadth for the evaluation of Establishment Clause challenges to government school-aid programs." 120 S. Ct. at 2556. Justice O'Connor's concurring opinion shows disagreement not only with the "expansive scope of the plurality's rule[,]" but with two specific aspects of its analysis. Id. First, she found the plurality's "treatment of neutrality comes close to assigning that factor singular importance in the future adjudication of Establishment Clause challenges to government school-aid programs." Id. Second, she found "the plurality's approval of actual diversion of government aid to religious indoctrination is in tension with our precedents and . . . unnecessary to decide the instant case." Id.

While agreeing with Justice Thomas that "neutrality is an important reason for upholding government-aid programs against Establishment Clause challenges," Justice O'Connor opined that "neutrality is not alone sufficient to qualify the aid as constitutional." 120 S. Ct at 2557–58. She criticized Justice Thomas's opinion for relying on logic which would support direct government aid to religious organizations based on the number of persons belonging to each organization. "[T]he plurality opinion foreshadows the approval of direct monetary subsidies to religious organizations, even when they use the money to advance their religious objectives." Id. at 2560. Justice O'Connor rejected an outright ban on any diversion of government funds to sectarian uses, but would enact a rule which requires plaintiffs to prove that the aid in question is, or has been, used for religious purposes, and found that "presumptions of religious indoctrination are normally inappropriate when evaluating neutral school-aid programs under the Establishment Clause." Id. at 2567.

Justice O'Connor concluded that because the school-aid program in Agostini was similar to that at issue in Mitchell, the Agostini criteria should control the outcome of the case; however, she noted that the "school-aid cases often pose difficult questions at the intersection of the neutrality and no-aid principles and therefore defy simple categorization under either rule." 120 S. Ct. at 2560.

In regard to Mitchell and its sharply divided plurality, we note that "[w]hen a fragmented Court decides a case and no single rationale explaining the result enjoys the assent of five Justices, 'the holding of the Court may be viewed as that position taken by those Members who concurred in the judgments on the narrowest grounds.'" *Marks v. United States,* 430 U.S. 188, 193 (1977) (quoting *Gregg v. Georgia,* 428 U.S. 153, 169 n.15(1976)). Accordingly, we find that the opinion of Justice O'Connor is the narrower of the plurality, as it utilizes the standard of Agostini based on a factual similarity rather than creating a new standard centered on neutrality, thereby making its mandates controlling.

III

We now apply the framework established by precedent to the case before us, recognizing the predominating theme in this area of law to be the need for careful judicial attention to the factual detail in the challenged statutory scheme.

At the outset, we note that Defendants' argument concerning other options available to Cleveland parents such as the Community Schools is at best irrelevant. Analyzing the scholarship program choices as compared to choices or schools outside the program is asking this Court to examine the entire context of Ohio education. Such a question is not before this Court. The

Defendants' argument would rewrite the law to require that the courts look to all possible alternatives to a challenged program, thus visiting issues of legislative choice and educational policy which no plaintiff has raised.

At oral argument, Defendants asserted repeatedly that the Community Schools program should be considered coterminous with the voucher program, arguing that the programs are merely separate sections in the statute. However, the statutory record does not support this argument, except for perhaps the literal meaning that the two programs do indeed occupy separate sections in the Ohio Code. The school voucher program is enacted as a complete program in the Ohio Revised Code. See Ohio Rev. Code §§3313.974–3313.983. The program is enacted as a part of the chapter on Boards of Education. See Ohio Rev. Code §3313.01 et seq. Furthermore, the school voucher program, and only the school voucher program, was challenged by Plaintiffs in this lawsuit. In contrast, the Community Schools program is codified in its own chapter. See Ohio Rev. Code §§3314.01 et seq. It is similarly a complete program within the Code: the statutory provisions govern all aspects of the program without reference to the voucher program. We may not view these two programs as inextricably interdependent when the plain language of the statutory scheme demonstrates the opposite. It is simply not the proper role of the courts to change statutory construction by judicial fiat. See *Brogan v. United States*, 522 U.S. 398, 408 (1998); *Nat'l Life and Accident Ins. Co. v. United States*, 524 F.2d 559, 560 (6th Cir.1975) ("The Courts . . . do not have the power to repeal or amend the enactments of the legislature even though they may disagree with the result; rather it is their function to give the natural and plain meaning effect to statutes. . . ."). Should we consider the Community Schools program in our analysis of the constitutionality of the school voucher program, we would open the door to a wide-reaching analysis which would permit us to consider any and all scholarship programs available to children who qualify for the school voucher program: we would be considering and comparing every available option for Cleveland children. Such an analysis would expand our jurisdiction far beyond the case at hand; we are presented only with the question of whether the school voucher program violates the Establishment Clause, and we must limit ourselves to that issue, regardless of the temptations Defendants' arguments present.

We find that Nyquist governs our result. Factually, the program at hand is a tuition grant program for low-income parents whose children attend private school parallel to the tuition reimbursement program found impermissible in Nyquist. Under both the New York statute in Nyquist, as well as the Ohio Statute at issue, parents receive government funds, either in direct payment for private school tuition or as a reimbursement for the same, and in both cases, the great majority of schools benefitted by these tuition dollars are sectarian. The Nyquist Court itself found there to be no distinction between "a reimbursement, a reward, or a subsidy, [as in all three,] the substantive impact is still the same." 413 U.S. at 786. As in Nyquist, the Ohio program contains no "effective means of guaranteeing that the state aid derived from public funds will be used exclusively for secular, neutral, and nonideological purposes." Id. at 780. Here, there is clearly "no endeavor to guarantee the separation between secular and religious functions and to ensure that State financial aid supports only the former." Id. at 783. In both Nyquist and this case, there are no restrictions on the religious schools as to their use of the tuition funds—the funds may be used for religious instruction or materials as easily as for erasers and playground equipment.

Despite the language of the statute, there is no evidence that the tuition vouchers serve as a neutral form of state assistance which would excuse the direct funding of religious institutions by the state, despite the statute's language. Admittedly, the voucher program does not restrict entry into the program to religious or sectarian schools, but facial neutrality alone does not bring state action into compliance with the First Amendment. See *Church of the Lukumi Bablu Aye, Inc. v. City of Hialeah*, 508 U.S. 520, 534 (1993). The school voucher program is not neutral in that it discourages the participation by schools not funded by religious institutions, and the Cleveland program limits the schools to which a parent can apply the voucher funds to those within the program. Practically speaking, the tuition restrictions mandated by the statute limit the ability of nonsectarian schools to participate in the program, as religious schools often have lower overhead costs, supplemental income from private donations, and consequently lower tuition needs. See Martha Minow, Reforming School Reform, 68 Fordham L. Rev. 257, 262 (1999)(finding that voucher funding levels typically "approximate[] the tuition level set by parochial schools [which] reflects subsidies from other sources"). In fact, Defendants admit that there is incentive for private nonsectarian schools to participate in the community schools program rather than in the school voucher program. See Brief of State at 10. The evidence illustrates this point in that 82% of participating schools are sectarian, just as in Nyquist where 85% of the participating schools were sectarian. Beyond that, we note that the number of available places for students in sectarian schools is higher than 82%, as many of the sectarian schools are larger and provide a greater number of places for children in the voucher program. Moreover, close to 96% of the students enrolled in the program for the 1999–2000 school year attended sectarian institutions.

The alleged choice afforded both public and private school participants in this program is illusory in that the program's design does not result in the participation of the adjacent public schools from outside the Cleveland school district. Per pupil expenditures in the public schools are backed by $7,097 in public funding. See Brief of Senel Taylor Intervenors at 17. At a maximum of $2,250, there is a financial disincentive for public schools outside the district to take on students via the school voucher program. Since its inception, no public schools from outside Cleveland have registered in the school voucher program, and there are no spaces available for children who wish to attend a suburban public school in place of a private school under the program. Therefore, the program clearly has the impermissible effect of promoting sectarian schools.

This is not the type of case which would fall into the exception to the Nyquist rules. Here, state assistance is only available to those students who attend private schools—the aid is clearly dependent on whether parents choose public or private schools. That the majority of places available in the program are for students attending sectarian schools is not unpersuasive. This program provides incentives for parents to choose schools other than mainstream public ones, but that choice does not extend to schools outside of the program. Students may not choose to attend community or magnet schools using a voucher, they may not apply a voucher to tuition at a private school outside the Cleveland School District, and they may not receive a voucher for a private school within the Cleveland School District which has not registered as part of the program. Rather, the program provides financial assistance for those parents who wish to place their children in the particular private schools, mostly religious, which take part in the program. We find such a scheme directly akin to Nyquist's offensive aid to only private school students, and not an instance where "the class of beneficiaries included all schoolchildren, those in public as well as those in private schools." 413 U.S. at 782 n.38. The effect of this program, like Nyquist and unlike Mueller and subsequent cases, is one where "public assistance amounting to tuition grants was provided only to parents of children in nonpublic schools." Mueller, 463 U.S. at 398.

Contrary to the tax deduction generally available in Mueller, the Ohio voucher program is available to curtail only those expenses which students attending certain private schools accrue. See 463 U.S. at 398 (distinguishing the Mueller program from that in Nyquist because in Nyquist, "tuition grants [were] provided only to parents of children in nonpublic schools"). The idea of parental choice as a determining factor which breaks a government–church nexus is inappropriate in the context of government limitation of the available choices to overwhelmingly sectarian private schools which can afford the tuition restrictions placed upon them and which have registered with the program. The absence of any meaningful public school choice from the decision matrix yields a limited and restricted palette for parents which is solely caused by state legislative structuring.

In contradistinction to Witters, a student under the Ohio statute cannot apply state aid to any school he or she chooses, including public schools, since under the Ohio program, no public schools have enrolled, nor are likely to enroll. Similarly, Agostini is inapposite because the services made available to students at parochial schools through the placement of public school teachers to teach secular subjects were available to all qualifying students without regard to the nature of the institution they attended. 521 U.S. at 232 (finding that under the New York program at issue in Agostini, and unlike the Nyquist program, services "are available to all children who meet the Act's eligibility requirements no matter . . . where they go to school). While the program upheld in Mitchell provided for the loan of instructional equipment by state agencies to both public and private schools, in this case aid predominantly flows directly to the coffers of religious institutions. Unlike Mitchell, under the Ohio statute, there are not "numerous private citizens who are free to direct the aid elsewhere" as the majority of the choices available to parents and students are religious institutions. 120 S. Ct. at 2533 (Thomas, J. plurality). The voucher program at issue constitutes the type of "direct monetary subsidies to religious institutions," that Justice O'Connor found impermissible in Mitchell. Id. at 2559–60 (O'Connor, J. concurring). This program is dissimilar to that upheld in both Agostini and Mitchell, as here aid goes only to students enrolled in private schools, thereby fostering the type of government entanglement prohibited under the Establishment Clause.

To approve this program would approve the actual diversion of government aid to religious institutions in endorsement of religious education, something "in tension" with the precedents of the Supreme Court. Mitchell, 120 S. Ct. at 2556. We find that when, as here, the government has established a program which does not permit private citizens to direct government aid freely as is their private choice, but which restricts their choice to a panoply of religious institutions and spaces with only a few alternative possibilities, then the Establishment Clause is violated. This scheme involves the grant of state aid directly and predominantly to the coffers of the private, religious schools, and it is unquestioned that these institutions incorporate religious concepts, motives, and themes into all facets of their educational planning. There is no neutral aid when that aid principally flows to religious institutions; nor is there truly "private choice" when the available choices resulting from the program design are predominantly religious.

We conclude that unlike Mitchell, Agostini, Witters and Mueller, the Ohio scholarship program is designed in a manner calculated to attract religious institutions and chooses the beneficiaries of aid by non-neutral criteria. The effect of the voucher program is in direct contravention to these Supreme Court cases which mandate that the state aid be neutrally available to all students who qualify, that the parents receiving the state aid have the option of applying the funds to secular organizations or causes as well as to religious institutions, and that the state aid does not provide an incentive to choose a religious institution over a secular institution. Accordingly, we hold that no genuine issue of material fact remains for trial that the voucher program has the primary effect of advancing religion, and that it constitutes an endorsement of religion and sectarian education in violation of the Establishment Clause. We therefore affirm the district court's order granting summary judgment to Plaintiffs.

IV

Intervenor Taylor asserts that the district court erred by holding that the Ohio Supreme Court's opinion in *Simmons-Harris v. Goff,* 711 N.E.2d 203 (Ohio 1999), did not estop Plaintiffs' claim, and by refusing to certify the question of estoppel to the Ohio Supreme Court. This Court reviews the issue of collateral estoppel as part of the summary judgment determination de novo. This Court reviews the district court's denial of certification for an abuse of discretion. See *Transamerica Ins. Co v. Duro Bag Mfg. Co.,* 50 F.3d 370, 372 (6th Cir. 1995).

Under both federal and state law, an "issue must have been necessary to support the judgment . . . in the prior proceeding" in order to find collateral estoppel. *Knox County Educ. Ass'n v. Knox County Bd. of Educ.,* 158 F.3d 361, 376–77 (6th Cir. 1998); accord *MetroHealth Med. Ctr. v. Hoffmann-LaRoche, Inc.,* 685 N.E.2d 529, 533 (Ohio 1997) ("Issue preclusion precludes the relitigation of an issue that has been actually and necessarily litigated and determined in a prior action."); cf. *Ameigh v. Baycliffs Corp.,* 690 N.E.2d 872, 875 (Ohio 1998)("Where the judgment of a court is not dispositive on issues which a party later seeks to litigate, res judicata is not applicable . . . even if the prior court decision has discussed the issues that are the subject of the current litigation."). A determination is not essential to the judgment if the judgment could be supported by an adequate and independent state ground. See *Lambrix v. Singletary,* 520 U.S. 518 522–24 (1997). In Goff, the Ohio Supreme Court held that the 1995 school voucher program was enacted in violation of the one-subject rule of the Ohio Constitution, and on that basis, ordered the program in its entirety "stricken" from the Ohio statute books. 711 N.E.2d at 203. That ruling entitled the plaintiffs to the relief they requested, and therefore, any discussion of other grounds for striking or upholding the statute could be neither necessary nor essential to the holding. The Ohio Court determined that the entire program could not stand; therefore, any analysis as to the constitutionality of particular portions of the program was by definition advisory or dicta, and cannot be relied upon to bar further litigation. Because Plaintiffs would not be able to obtain Supreme Court review of the Ohio Supreme Court's determination as to the Establishment Clause, such determinations cannot constitute collateral estoppel. See *Cal. v. Rooney,* 483 U.S. 307, 311 (1987) (declining to review a Fourth Amendment ruling adverse to the state of California where that ruling was unnecessary to a judgment in favor of the state).

Similarly, the district court did not err in refusing to certify the question to the Ohio Supreme Court. The governing law as to whether a party is estopped from relitigating an issue not essential to the court's determination is clear and uncontroverted; we therefore find no abuse of discretion in the district court's determination.

V

Before concluding, we must pause to briefly address the dissent, not for the purpose of dignifying its hyperbole, but to quash any putatively substantive argument which may have found its way through the gratuitous insults. The dissent first makes the bald-faced assertion that the majority has struck down the voucher program as unconstitutional without any "meaningful" independent analysis, and that the majority simply concludes that the program is "foreordained" to be found unconstitutional under Nyquist. According to the dissent, the New York statute in Nyquist is "totally different" from the Ohio statute before us today, thus making it impossible to "take seriously" the majority's conclusion that Nyquist is controlling. However, even a cursory reading of the majority opinion clearly indicates that it is the dissent and its rhetoric which should not be taken seriously. As carefully set forth in Part III of this opinion, the Ohio statute at issue has the same effect as that of the New York statute held unconstitutional under the Establishment Clause in Nyquist. Both statutes have the impermissible effect of benefitting only students in particular private, and mostly religious, schools, irrespective of the illusory choice provided on the face of the Ohio statute. The fact that the dissent may not agree with the analysis set forth in the opinion to illustrate this point does not ispo facto render the analysis "meaningless."

Second, in a similar vein, the dissent claims that the majority reaches its conclusion that the voucher program is unconstitutional under the Establishment Clause without conducting any "meaningful" analysis into the Supreme Court's several cases on this issue since Nyquist was handed down. However, in Part II of this opinion, the majority painstakingly sets forth First Amendment Establishment Clause jurisprudence and its evolution since Nyquist, while carefully applying that law to the statute at hand in the following section. Again, it is obvious that the dissent's bald-faced assertion that this analysis is not "meaningful" is apparently born out of nothing more than its disagreement with the outcome of this case, rather than with an objective observation. It is the majority which employs the evolving jurisprudential standards in reaching its outcome, while the dissent employs a rigid antiquated standard to reach its result driven outcome in contravention of the Supreme Court's latest pronouncements.(1) See, e.g., Agostini, 521 U.S. at 222–26.

VI

We recognize the importance of this case and the precedential value it espouses. Equally as important, we are aware of the critical nature of questions of educational policy, and the need to establish successful schools and academic programs for children. We find, however, that even more important is the need to uphold the Constitution of the United States and, in this case, to override the State of Ohio's statutory scheme where it constitutes an impermissible infringement under the Establishment Clause of the First Amendment. We therefore AFFIRM the district court's order finding the school voucher program unconstitutional, as well as the court's determination that Plaintiffs are not collaterally estopped.

Concurring in Part, Dissenting in Part

RYAN, Circuit Judge, concurring in part and dissenting in part. My colleagues' resolution of the question presented by the plaintiffs' collateral estoppel claim is eminently correct and so I join part IV of the court's opinion. However, because I believe Ohio's voucher program to be constitutional under the First Amendment and the Supreme Court's Establishment Clause cases interpreting the amendment, I must respectfully dissent from the majority's treatment of the voucher program's constitutionality.

My brothers have struck down as unconstitutional Ohio's effort to establish a school-choice voucher program whose primary purpose is to enable mostly minority poverty-level school children, in Cleveland, Ohio, to escape the devastating consequences of attending Cleveland's demonstrably failed public schools. My colleagues have done so not on the basis of any independent constitutional analysis of the Ohio Pilot Project Scholarship Program, as the voucher program is formally known, but because they claim the invalidity of the statute is a conclusion foreordained by the United States Supreme Court's decision in *Committee for Public Education and Religious Liberty v. Nyquist,* 413 U.S. 756 (1973). I disagree. The New York statute interpreted in Nyquist and the Ohio statute before us are totally different in all of their essential respects, both in their purposes and their provisions for carrying out their respective purposes. It is impossible to take seriously the majority's claim that Nyquist governs our result and, for that reason, requires that the Ohio voucher program must be struck down.

Moreover, the majority's refusal to conduct any meaningful analysis of the Supreme Court's several Establishment Clause decisions handed down in the 27 years since Nyquist was decided, its insistence that the plainly distinguishable Nyquist case is directly on point, and the factually unsupported antireligious-schools arguments in the opinion strongly suggest that the majority has simply signed onto the familiar anti-voucher mantra that voucher programs are no more than a scheme to funnel public funds into religious schools.

I

According to the majority, this court need not conduct any independent analysis whether Ohio's voucher program violates the Establishment Clause because Nyquist is "on point with the matter at hand." Slip op. at 13. In my judgment, the majority is mistaken as a matter of fact (the two statutes are totally different) and as a matter of law (the relevant Establishment Clause jurisprudence has changed since Nyquist). As to the latter, a reading of the Supreme Court's Establishment Clause cases decided since 1973 makes it unmistakably clear that the voucher program passes constitutional muster. I do not claim that the Nyquist decision has been overruled, although some of the reasoning in the Nyquist opinion has been "undermined," as the Ohio Supreme Court put it in *Simmons-Harris v. Goff,* 711 N.E.2d 203, 208 (Ohio 1999); Nyquist is simply inapposite to the appeal before us.

The New York statutory provisions struck down in Nyquist and the Ohio voucher program are essentially different laws; they are plainly distinguishable both in their declared purposes and in the manner of their application. For that reason alone, the reasoning and the holding of the Nyquist decision cannot govern our result.

A

I begin with a comparison of the New York statutory provisions construed in Nyquist and the Ohio statute before us; a comparison that shows very clearly that the two laws are essentially different. I then examine the Supreme Court Establishment Clause cases decided since Nyquist, which clearly indicate that the Ohio voucher program is not unconstitutional.

1

In Nyquist, the Supreme Court was required to decide whether a New York statute containing provisions for both direct and indirect financial assistance to New York's private schools violated the Establishment Clause. The statute provided for three forms of assistance: (1) direct grants for building maintenance and repairs for private school buildings; (2) tuition reimbursement grants for some low-income parents of children already attending the private schools; and (3) a form of tax relief for parents who failed to qualify for tuition reimbursement under the statute. See Nyquist, 413 U.S. at 762–65.

The New York legislature enacted the statute for the sole purpose of directly benefitting New York state's 2,038 financially pressed private schools, wherein some 700,000–800,000 students—almost 20% of the state's entire elementary and secondary school population—were being educated. See id. at 768. The legislative "findings" in the New York statute declared: (1) it was in the state's interest to provide funding for "maintenance and repair" of the state's private schools in order to protect the health and safety of those attending the schools; (2) the state had an interest in promoting "alternative educational systems"; and (3) a "precipitous decline" in the number of children attending private schools would perpetuate an already existing fiscal crisis in public schools. Id. at 763–65.

The Nyquist Court held that the New York law offended the Establishment Clause because "the effect of the aid [was] unmistakably to provide desired financial support for nonpublic, sectarian institutions." Id. at 783. Furthermore, the Nyquist Court concluded that "[i]n the absence of an effective means of guaranteeing that the state aid derived from public funds will be used exclusively for secular, neutral, and nonideological purposes, it is clear from our cases that direct aid in whatever form is invalid." Id. at 780.

The Ohio voucher program, which is adequately described in the majority opinion, could not be more unlike the New York statute both in its purpose and in the manner of its application. The essential differences between the New York and Ohio statutes may be summarized as follows:

First, the purpose of the New York statute was to provide financial help to New York's financially troubled private schools because their closing would force New York's public schools to absorb the private school students, resulting in massive increased costs and the related burdens of absorbing as many as three quarters of a million new students.

The purpose of the Ohio statute, on the other hand, is to provide financial help to poverty-level students attending the public schools in Cleveland in order to enable them, if they wish, to attend nonreligious private schools, religious private schools, public schools in neighboring districts that wish to participate in the voucher program, or to obtain special tutoring while remaining in the Cleveland public schools.

Second, the New York program involved direct financial grants to New York's private schools, religious and nonreligious, primarily for maintenance and repair. Although the tuition reimbursement and tax relief sections of the statute appeared to benefit the parents of private school children, the Nyquist Court stated that the "tuition reimbursement program also fails the 'effect' test, for much the same reasons that govern its maintenance and repair grants." Id.

Under the Ohio voucher program, on the other hand, there is no provision for any financial grants in any form to any private schools. A voucher recipient receives a scholarship check, and the funds therefrom reach a private religious school only after a child's parents have considered a variety of options available to them and have chosen the religious private school as the best option for their child.

Third, the New York statute permitted government aid to schools that discriminated against children on the basis of religion and, in fact, several qualifying schools imposed religious restrictions on admissions. See id. at 767–68.

The Ohio voucher program, on the other hand, contains a provision explicitly forbidding participating schools from discriminating against prospective students on the basis of religion. See Ohio Rev. Code §3313.976(A)(4).

It is clear that the New York statute struck down in Nyquist and the Ohio statute before us are dissimilar laws both in their purposes and the methodologies for carrying out their purposes. As the majority acknowledges, "[a] single factual difference consequently can serve to entangle or free a particular governmental practice from the reach of the [Establishment] Clause's constitutional prohibition." Slip op. at __ (internal quotation marks and citation omitted). A case construing a statute so manifestly different than the one before us could hardly, as a factual matter, be a binding precedent on this court.

2

The substantial differences in the purpose and application of the two statutes is not the only reason Nyquist does not govern our result. The additional reason is that the rule of law upon which Nyquist was decided has changed. First, the Nyquist era categorical prohibition against direct grants to aid religious schools is no longer the law; and second, the criteria for determining when a statute has the forbidden "primary effect" of advancing religion have been modified.

In *Lemon v. Kurtzman*, 403 U.S. 602 (1971), the Supreme Court fashioned the following test for assessing whether a statute violates the Establishment Clause:

First, the statute must have a secular legislative purpose; second, its principal or primary effect must be one that neither advances nor inhibits religion. . . , finally, the statute must not foster an excessive government entanglement with religion.

Id. at 612–13 (emphasis added) (internal quotation marks and citation omitted).

The Nyquist Court ruled that the New York statute violated the Lemon test because it had the "impermissible effect of advancing religion." Nyquist, 413 U.S. at 794. It did so, the Court said, by providing direct financial assistance to religious schools without any restrictions as to the schools' use of the funds, therefore "advanc[ing] the religious mission of sectarian schools." Id. at 779–80. But three years ago in *Agostini v. Felton,* 521 U.S. 203 (1997), the Supreme Court declared unmistakably that "we have departed from the rule . . . that all government aid that directly assists the educational function of religious schools is invalid." Id. at 225. The Agostini Court then proceeded to redefine and narrow the criteria for determining when government aid that finds its way to a religious school has the primary effect of advancing religion.

Again, I do not question for a moment the correctness of the Supreme Court's decision in Nyquist. I accept it both analytically and precedentially as a faithful 1973 application of the "primary effect" test of Lemon. However, Nyquist was not analyzed and decided under what the Agostini Court called its "changed . . . understanding of the criteria used to assess whether aid to religion has an impermissible effect." Id. at 223. Since this appeal is also an "impermissible effect" case, our decision cannot be controlled by Nyquist.

B

What then is the Supreme Court's "changed ... understanding" of the proper test for determining whether a law has the primary effect of advancing religion?

In *Mueller v. Allen,* 463 U.S. 388 (1983), the Court held that a Minnesota statute authorizing a tax deduction for certain educational expenses for parents of students attending either public or private schools, religious or nonreligious, did not violate the "impermissible effect" prong of the Lemon test. The Court focused on the fact that the deduction was given directly to the parents, without regard to the type of school, religious or nonreligious, to which the parents might choose to send their children, as a strong indicator of the statute's "neutrality." See id. at 397–400. Any money received at a religious school, the Court said, was "ultimately controlled by the private choices of individual parents." Id. at 400.

This principle—that whether public funds find their way to a religious school is of no constitutional consequence if they get there as a result of genuinely private choice—was reasserted in *Witters v. Washington Department of Services for the Blind,* 474 U.S. 481 (1986). There, a Washington state program survived an Establishment Clause challenge even though it provided vocational rehabilitation assistance for a blind individual to attend a Christian college in order to study to be a Christian pastor. Funds under the program were dispersed directly to the eligible applicants who made the choice of where to expend the educational funds; therefore, "[a]ny aid ... that ultimately flow[ed] to religious institutions [did] so only as a result of the genuinely independent and private choices of aid recipients." Id. at 488.

In *Zobrest v. Catalina Foothills School District,* 509 U.S. 1 (1993), the Court upheld the constitutionality of a program providing a sign-language interpreter for a deaf student in a Catholic high school. Relying upon Witters and Mueller, the Zobrest Court concluded that the statute gave parents the choice of where to send their eligible children to school and "distributes benefits neutrally ... without regard to the 'sectarian–nonsectarian, or public–nonpublic nature' of the school." Id. at 10 (quoting Witters, 474 U.S. at 487).

This line of cases culminated in the Agostini decision in 1997, in which the Supreme Court declared that its understanding of the criteria for determining whether, in any specific program, government aid has the primary effect of advancing religion had "changed." Indeed, in Agostini the Supreme Court went so far as to modify the Lemon test it had relied upon in Nyquist. The Agostini Court began by recasting Lemon's "entanglement" inquiry as a factor under the "impermissible effect" prong rather than as a separate and independent criterion. See Agostini, 521 U.S. at 232–34. It then identified three new sub-criteria to consider when evaluating whether a government-aid program violates Lemon's "impermissible effect" prong. These are:

(1) whether the aid results in governmental indoctrination;
(2) whether the aid program defines its recipients by reference to religion; and
(3) whether the aid creates an excessive entanglement between government and religion.

See id. at 234.

Using this modified Lemon test, the Agostini Court found constitutional a federally mandated New York program that sent public school teachers into private parochial schools to provide remedial education to eligible children. Under the program, children meeting the eligibility requirements received the services, whether they attended a private or public school. See id. at 232. The Agostini Court concluded that programs in which money ultimately flows to a private, religious school based on the " 'genuinely independent and private choices of' individuals" do not violate the Establishment Clause. Id. at 226 (quoting Witters, 474 U.S. at 488).

Finally, in *Mitchell v. Helms,* 120 S. Ct. 2530 (2000), a plurality opinion written by Justice Thomas, the Court upheld the constitutionality of a federally mandated Louisiana program where educational materials were loaned to public and private schools, both religious and nonreligious. Justice Thomas emphasized that the statute did not have an "impermissible effect" because the "principles of neutrality and private choice, and their relationship to each other [that] were [also] prominent" in the Court's decisions in Agostini, Zobrest, Witters, and Mueller were present. Id. at 2542.

II

It is against this background of changed Supreme Court Establishment Clause jurisprudence that we must test the constitutionality of the Ohio voucher program.

The Ohio statute is the product of a 1994 order issued by the United States District Court in Cleveland, directing the Ohio Superintendent of Education to address the educational crisis in Cleveland's public schools. See *Reed v. Rhodes,* 869 F.Supp. 1274 (N.D. Ohio 1994). The Ohio legislature and the state's governor responded with the voucher program that is before us today. See Ohio Rev. Code §§3313.974–3313.979. We may safely assume that in fashioning the new law, the Ohio legislators and the governor knew that the challenge they faced was to design a law that would survive a federal constitutional challenge on Establishment Clause grounds. That is not to say that the statute the legislators wrote and the governor signed into law is insulated from federal judicial constitutional scrutiny. Rather, it is to say what the majority does not even acknowledge: this statute is presumed to be constitutional. See *McDonald v. Board of Election Comm'rs,* 394 U.S. 802, 809 (1969); *Hartford Fire Ins. Co. v. Lawrence, Dykes, Goodenberger, Bower & Clancy,* 740 F.2d 1362, 1366 (6th Cir. 1984). This presumption is not a mere literary figure for rote recitation in all appellate opinions addressing the constitutionality of legislative enactments; it is a bedrock rule of statutory construction, one we are bound assiduously to honor as we begin our assessment of the validity of the Ohio statute.

The first of the Lemon criteria that must be met if a statute is to survive an Establishment Clause challenge is that it have a "secular purpose." The Ohio voucher program meets this criterion and the plaintiffs agree that it does. The sole purpose of the voucher program is to save Cleveland's mostly poor, mostly minority, public school children from the devastating consequences of requiring them to remain in the failed Cleveland schools, if they wish to escape. There is also no serious claim that the statute is constitutionally invalid solely because it fosters an "excessive entanglement" between government and religion. Rather, the only issue in the case is whether the voucher program has the forbidden "primary effect" of advancing religion. This court's first duty, therefore, after recognizing that Nyquist's factually and legally outdated decision is of no help, is to proceed to examine the first two criteria from Agostini's "impermissible effect" test to determine whether the effect of Ohio's voucher program is to advance religion, either because (1) the aid it provides results in governmental indoctrination, or (2) the program defines its recipients by reference to religion. See Agostini, 521 U.S. at 234. These are the only two issues properly before us.

A

In addressing Agostini's first criterion for testing a statute's claimed impermissible effect, we must ask whether the government aid in the form of the tuition voucher results in "governmental indoctrination." It is obvious that the Ohio statute does not have the remotest effect of providing governmental indoctrination in any religion, to say nothing of having such a primary effect.

The Supreme Court decisions since Lemon and Nyquist have emphasized that the critical question in determining whether government aid ultimately flowing to religious schools results in governmental indoctrination is if the recipient beneficiaries make a "genuinely independent and private choice[]" to "spend" the funds in a religious school. Id. at 226 (internal quotation marks and citation omitted). If the recipients have such an independent and private choice, then the government's decision to provide the money to fund that choice does not have the effect of advancing religion. The government is, of necessity, neutral in the matter. Implicit in that constitutional rule of law, as it applies in this case, is that there must be a genuine choice from among a range of alternatives that indicate complete neutrality on the part of the government as to where the recipient parents may choose to spend the government-aid funds. The voucher program does not offend the Establishment Clause because the statute allows parents to make a genuine choice for their children who are currently in Cleveland public schools.

What are the choices Ohio has given these Cleveland parents?

(1) To permit their children to remain in the Cleveland public schools as before;
(2) To accept a tuition voucher for them to attend a Cleveland area nonreligious private school;
(3) To accept a tuition voucher for them to attend a Cleveland area religious private school;
(4) To accept a voucher for them to obtain special tutorial help in the Cleveland schools; or
(5) To accept a voucher for them to attend a public school in a district adjacent to Cleveland, although for the present these districts have declined to participate in the program.

See Ohio Rev. Code §§3313.976–3313.978.

It is difficult to imagine a statute that could afford its voucher recipients a broader spectrum of educational choice. It is true, of course, that the public school districts adjacent to Cleveland have declined to participate in the voucher program, but there is not the slightest hint in the record that when the Ohio statute was enacted either the legislators or the governor had any idea that the public school districts adjacent to Cleveland would not participate. What we measure today is not whether the children in Cleveland have the fullest conceivable range of options available to them that a panel of federal judges might think to be ideal, but rather, whether the statute, as enacted, has the primary effect of advancing religion by involving the state in governmental indoctrination under Agostini's first criterion. See Mitchell, 120 S. Ct. at 2541–44. To my knowledge, no federal court has ever held that a school-choice voucher program is unconstitutional because the range of choices does not include a public school option; certainly the majority does not cite such a case.

B

Neither does the Ohio program "define its recipients by reference to religion," the second Agostini factor for testing for "impermissible effect." Agostini, 521 U.S. at 234. The program defines the first-priority voucher recipients by reference to (1) their attendance in one of Cleveland's public schools; and (2) a family income that is not more than 200 percent of the federally established poverty level. See Ohio Rev. Code §3313.978(A). And the statute explicitly forbids a religious test for admission to a participating school, including religious schools. See id. at §3313.976(A)(4). A parent has the choice of using the voucher in a private religious school, a private nonreligious school, for tutoring in the public school, or in a public school in a neighboring district if any wish to participate. The statute expresses no preference, explicitly or implicitly, either as to the religion of the voucher recipients, or if the recipient chooses a private school, whether the voucher is applied to a religious or nonreligious school.

The Agostini Court recognized, of course, that the eligibility requirements of a government-aid program could "have the effect of advancing religion by creating a financial incentive to undertake religious indoctrination." Agostini, 521 U.S. at 231. The Court noted that a financial incentive to choose a religious school over a nonreligious school is not present "where the aid is allocated on the basis of neutral, secular criteria that neither favor nor disfavor religion, and is made available to both religious and secular beneficiaries on a nondiscriminatory basis." Id.

Despite the plain evidence that the aid to the parents of the Cleveland school children is indeed "allocated on the basis of neutral, secular criteria that neither favor nor disfavor religion, and is made available to both religious and secular beneficiaries on a nondiscriminatory basis," id., the majority continues to insist that the voucher program is not neutral because it creates a forbidden "incentive" for parents in Cleveland to choose a religious school. As best I can understand it, they rest this conclusion—unsupported though it is by any evidence in the record—on two further conclusions. The first is that because the vast majority—82 percent—of the private schools participating in the Ohio program are religious, the people of Cleveland are denied a "genuine" choice. This absurd argument is made despite the indisputable fact that of all the private nonreligious private schools participating in the program, not one has ever turned away a voucher applicant for any reason. This not very thinly veiled antipathy the majority has shown toward religious schools—its argument that there are too many religious schools in the program—is meritless for another reason: the Supreme Court has flatly rejected the argument that a high percentage of religious schools participating in a government-aid program is an indicator that the government is engaging in governmental indoctrination of religion. See Mitchell, 120 S. Ct. at 2542; id. at 2562 (O'Connor, J., concurring); Agostini, 521 U.S. at 229; Mueller, 463 U.S. at 401.

Second, the majority then attempts to arouse support for its view that the Ohio statute creates a forbidden incentive for parents to choose a religious school by utilizing the shamefully transparent argument that this statute should be struck down because the religious schools in the program are too religious. In support of this proposition, the majority devotes considerable attention to the mission statements of several religious schools, which indicate the pervasively religious character of their programs. My brothers conclude therefrom that these schools "believe in interweaving religious beliefs with secular subjects" and "incorporate [in their curriculum] religious concepts, motives, and themes." Slip op. at 5, 27. Imagine, religious schools that are truly religious!

This plainly hostile attack on the religious schools in the Ohio voucher program is one I would of [sic] thought unworthy of mention in an opinion from this great court. Is the point being made here that religious schools may participate in a voucher program providing they are not too religious? Or, is it that these poverty-level parents in Cleveland cannot be trusted to understand what they will be exposing their children to if they choose one of these religious schools? One would have thought that the nail was long ago driven into the coffin bearing the discredited arguments that if a voucher program involved too many religious schools, or if those involved are honestly, genuinely, and essentially religious, the statute is therefore invalid as "advancing religion." This most unattractive argument was utterly rejected in Witters, 474 U.S. at 486–88, and Mueller, 463 U.S. at 397–400, and was rejected in Justice Powell's concurring opinion in Witters. See Witters, 474 U.S. at 492 (Powell, J., concurring). Moreover, Justice Thomas, writing for a clear majority on this point in Mitchell, stated:

In short, nothing in the Establishment Clause requires the exclusion of pervasively sectarian schools from otherwise permissible aid programs, and other doctrines of this Court bar it. This doctrine, born of bigotry, should be buried now.

Mitchell, 120 S. Ct. at 2552.

The majority, in this case, straining mightily to strike down this law, then conjures still another anti-voucher argument (the reader will recall that the majority's decisional premise is that this case is controlled by Nyquist and, implicitly, that all else is irrelevant).

My colleagues' next non-Nyquist argument is that the "school voucher program is not neutral in that it discourages the participation by schools not funded by religious institutions." Slip op. at 23. This statement in the majority opinion, which, like so many others in the opinion, is totally without any basis in the evidence, is then fortified by my brothers' ipse dixit that "religious schools often have lower overhead costs, supplemental income from private donations, and consequently lower tuition needs." Id. at 24. The only authority my colleagues offer for this speculation is a Fordham University Law Review article. I can only surmise that the point my colleagues wish to make here is that nonreligious schools will not participate in Ohio's voucher program because the voucher will not cover the cost of educating a student in a nonreligious school. This, my brothers reason, creates an "incentive" for the parents to send their children to the religious schools where they can be educated more efficiently and for fewer dollars.

There is absolutely no evidence in the record to support the majority's argument that the Ohio statute creates a financial "disincentive" for Cleveland's neighboring, suburban public school districts to participate in the program. There is no evidence to support what the majority seems to imply—that those wishing to use a voucher choose not to do so because other Cleveland area public schools are not participating. Nor is there evidence that if a public school chooses to participate in the voucher program, it will lose its state funding.

These arguments are built on a "factual" predicate that has absolutely no basis in the record. There is not a scintilla of evidence in this case that any school, public or private, has been discouraged from participating in the school voucher program because it cannot "afford" to do so. The import of this argument, as best I can understand it, is that the parents of the Cleveland school children have an "incentive" to choose Cleveland's religious schools because there are not enough nonreligious schools participating in the program. Of course, there is no evidence of that either. And there is no evidence that any of the several nonreligious, private schools participating in the program have ever rejected a single voucher applicant for any reason, including a supposed inability to afford the theoretical differential between the value of a $2,500 voucher and the actual cost of a nonreligious, private school education.

While I hesitate to dignify the majority's speculation with speculation of my own, what is at stake in this case is too important to let any of my colleagues' meritless arguments go unanswered.

Since it is indisputable that no nonreligious, private school, or any other school for that matter, has ever been discouraged from participating in the Cleveland voucher program and no evidence that any private school, religious or nonreligious, has ever turned away a voucher applicant for any reason, what my colleagues must be getting at is even more insidious and offensive. The point apparently is that Cleveland parents would never choose to send their child to a religious school in Cleveland if they could afford to send their child to a nonreligious, private school, or another public school, but that they cannot do so because the cost differential between the value of a $2,500 voucher and the actual tuition of Cleveland's nonreligious, private schools is prohibitive. Again, it is of no small importance that there is absolutely no evidence in the record that any Cleveland public school parent has declined to enroll his or her child in a nonreligious, private school in Cleveland because there was a differential cost that was prohibitive. It is probably true that no private school, religious or nonreligious, can educate a child for the voucher value of $2,500. But, in all probability, the participating private schools are willing to accept the voucher as meeting a portion of the actual educational costs for these children and are willing to absorb the differential cost as part of their pro bono service in Cleveland to help save as many of these children as possible from the disastrous consequences of continuing in the city's failed public schools.

But more important than all of that speculation is the reality that the majority's "neutral only if affordable to all" test is utterly meritless as a matter of law because the now settled Establishment Clause jurisprudence is that whether aid is allocated on the basis of neutral, secular criteria is the key determinant of whether, having made the aid available, the state has engaged in governmental indoctrination in religion. See Agostini, 521 U.S. at 231.

If the simplicity and clarity of the Supreme Court's language in Agostini is not sufficient to demonstrate that the Ohio statute does not in any respect operate to advance religion, confirmatory language of crystal clarity appears in the Supreme Court's recent decision in Mitchell. In a passage in his opinion which enjoys the support of a majority of the Justices, and arguably even the support of the dissenters, Justice Thomas states:

[T]he question whether governmental aid to religious schools results in governmental indoctrination is ultimately a question whether any religious indoctrination that occurs in these schools could reasonably be attributed to governmental action.

Mitchell, 120 S. Ct. at 2541.

The line of cases decided in the Supreme Court beginning with Mueller in 1983 and ending with Mitchell in 2000 make it unmistakably clear that the majority's "impermissible incentive" argument has no basis in our Establishment Clause jurisprudence. The rule is now settled that a government program that permits financial aid ultimately to reach religious schools does not offend the Establishment Clause if the government's role in the program is neutral. Neutrality exists if the "governmental aid that goes to a religious institution does so 'only as a result of the genuinely independent and private choices of individuals'" Id. (quoting Agostini, 521 U.S. at 226). Justice Thomas wrote that "simply because an aid program offers private schools, and thus religious schools, a benefit that they did not previously receive does not mean that the program, by reducing the cost of securing a religious education, creates ... an 'incentive' for parents to choose such an education for their children." Id. at 2543–44. Finally, Justice Thomas concluded that the possibility that government aid might be diverted by a sectarian school towards some religious end is irrelevant, for Establishment Clause purposes, if the government aid program provides the aid in a neutral manner. See id. at 2547.

In her concurring opinion in Mitchell, Justice O'Connor, joined by Justice Breyer, agreed that "neutrality is an important reason for upholding government-aid programs" against Establishment Clause challenges, but she reiterated that it was just one factor to consider in challenges to government school-aid programs and not a "factor [of] singular importance." Id. at 2556–57 (O'Connor, J., concurring). Even Justice Souter's dissenting opinion, which Justices Stevens and Ginsburg joined, conceded that the Establishment Clause presents no obstacle to government aid if it reaches sectarian schools as a result of the private choices of aid recipients. See id. at 2584 (Souter, J., dissenting).

Justice O'Connor emphasized the distinction between "true private-choice programs" and "per-capita school-aid programs." Id. at 2559 (O'Connor, J., concurring). The Ohio voucher program, like the programs in Zobrest and Witters, is a true private-choice program because the aid is given directly to eligible individuals, who in turn decide where to spend it. The programs considered in Mitchell and Agostini were examples of per-capita school-aid programs because aid was distributed based on the number of students attending each school, regardless of whether the school was religiously based or not. Justice O'Connor concluded that true private-choice programs were more likely to survive Establishment Clause challenges, even though government aid was diverted to the religious schools, because "'[a]ny aid ... that ultimately flows to religious institutions does so only as a result of the genuinely independent and private choices of aid recipients.'" Id. at 2558 (quoting Witters, 474 U.S. at 488) (O'Connor, J., concurring).

True private-choice programs, by their very nature, cannot have the forbidden "primary effect" of the government "advancing religion" because the aid is given directly to the beneficiary and that student or parent retains control over where the aid will be applied. "The fact that aid flows to the religious school and is used for the advancement of religion is therefore wholly dependent on the student's private decision." Id. at 2559. Furthermore, when government aid flows to a religious school as a result of "independent decisions made by numerous individuals ... , [n]o reasonable observer is likely to draw from the facts ... an inference that the State itself is endorsing a religious practice or belief." Id. (internal quotation marks and citation omitted).

The majority opinion in this case claims the voucher program "involves the grant of state aid directly and predominantly to the coffers of the private, religious schools." Slip op. at 27. Furthermore, according to the majority, "[t]here is no neutral aid when that aid principally flows to religious institutions. . . ." Id. at 27. The majority ignores that this view has been flat-out rejected by the Supreme Court in the decisions I have discussed which make it very clear that the number of religious schools participating in the voucher program, the thoroughness of the religious training that occurs there, and the use to which such schools might put the funds are all totally irrelevant to the question of the government's neutrality, when the government aid reaches a religious school only as a result of the recipient's " 'genuinely independent and private choice[].' " See Mitchell, 120 S. Ct. at 2541 (citation omitted); Zobrest, 509 U.S. at 8; Witters, 474 U.S. at 486. By ignoring the recent Supreme Court cases emphasizing the importance of genuinely independent and private choices and the distinction between true private-choice programs and per-capita school-aid programs, the majority has failed to conduct a "meaningful" independent analysis of the voucher program's constitutionality.

III

In summary, and to repeat, according to the Supreme Court, a true private-choice program does not result in "governmental indoctrination" so long as the path of the government aid is determined by the " 'genuinely independent and private choice[]' " of the aid recipients. See Mitchell, 120 S. Ct. at 2541 (citation omitted); id. at 2557–60 (O'Connor, J., concurring); Agostini, 521 U.S. at 226; Zobrest, 509 U.S. at 10, 12; Witters, 474 U.S. at 488; Mueller, 463 U.S. at 397–98, 400.

Ohio's voucher program easily meets this test. Before a voucher is "spent" at a religious school, Cleveland parents must independently make two important choices:

First, they must decide whether their child will take advantage of the voucher alternatives at all, or select another option, such as remaining in the Cleveland schools, undertaking home schooling, or attending one of Cleveland's well regarded community schools. Second, if a child's parents choose the voucher option, they must make the further "genuinely independent and private choice[]" whether to use the voucher at a private school, nonreligious or religious, or for special tutoring in the Cleveland public schools. The voucher-use choice of attending a public school in a neighboring district is not presently available to Cleveland parents because no neighboring district has opted into the voucher program.

It is difficult to imagine how a voucher statute could be crafted that more clearly and decisively forecloses the government from having any role in the religious indoctrination of Cleveland school children, or forecloses it from defining the recipients of the vouchers by reference to religion, than through the range of free and independent choices the statute gives to the parents whose children attend the Cleveland public schools.

IV

In striking down this statute today, the majority perpetuates the long history of lower federal court hostility to educational choice. It does so by reaching back to a 1973 Supreme Court decision, Nyquist, that construes a statute that is light years away from the voucher program before us and that rests upon law that has been altered in an important respect by subsequent Supreme Court decisions. My colleagues refuse to acknowledge that the program in Nyquist is factually distinguishable in essential ways from the Ohio voucher program and that the Supreme Court has explicitly declared that the criteria for determining whether a statute authorizing government aid to schools violates the Establishment Clause have changed. And then, almost as if recognizing that its Nyquist-is-directly-on-point argument cannot withstand close scrutiny, the majority resorts to the lamentable tactic of attempting to arouse support for its view by making the familiar but unworthy arguments that the voucher program has too many religious schools and that they are too religious. This tactic should fail, first, because it is rooted in nativist bigotry and, second, because it has been explicitly rejected by the Supreme Court as a legitimate determinant of whether a government is engaging in religious indoctrination.

Despite the majority's disclaimer that "courts do not make educational policy; we do not sit in omnipotent judgment as to the efficacy of one scheme or program versus another," slip op. at 9, the majority opinion is nothing more than an attack upon the philosophical and cultural desirability of publicly funded educational choice for the poor. This case and its result—sentencing nearly 4,000 poverty-level, mostly minority, children in Cleveland to return to the indisputably failed Cleveland public schools from which, in many cases, they escaped as long as three years ago—is an exercise in raw judicial power having no basis in the First Amendment or in the Supreme Court's Establishment Clause jurisprudence.

In all events, a matter of this gravity and of such immense importance to the Cleveland children who are directly affected, and indeed to the nation, should not be determined by just two judges of this court. Therefore, I respectfully urge my colleagues to take this case for en banc review, when they are asked to do so, and decide the vitally important Establishment Clause issue it presents, after giving careful consideration to the full panoply of Supreme Court Establishment Clause jurisprudence, and not just one, inapposite 1973 case.

As to what is written in part IV of the majority opinion, I have no disagreement.

Notes:

1. Judge Ryan inappropriately calls for an en banc review of the matter in his dissent. There are rules and procedures governing a call for en banc review once a case has been decided, whether the call is made by a party or sua sponte by an active judge of this Court or member of the original panel, and it is the process contemplated by these rules and procedures which should be used to invoke en banc review after the Court's opinion has been issued. See *Craft v. CIR*, Nos. 99-1734, 99-1737, 2000 WL 1726906, at n.18 (6th Cir. Nov. 22, 2000) (criticizing the concurring opinion's exhortation for en banc review of the matter, while noting that Fed. R. App. P. 35(b) and 6 Cir. I.O.P. 35(c) set forth the appropriate procedures to follow when calling for such review). The unfortunate practice of arguing for en banc review of a case in a panel member's separate opinion—instead of simply permitting the Court's regular operating procedures for seeking such review to be followed subsequent to the issuance of the majority opinion—is one which should not be perpetuated.

Background Materials on School Vouchers

Participants will find the following background materials on school vouchers useful in familiarizing themselves with the issues dealt with in the corresponding court case. These materials detail the history of the issue, related court cases that influence the debate, and the ways an eventual Supreme Court decision will likely affect the American public.

School Vouchers

By KATHY KOCH

It was one of the most anticipated Supreme Court decisions of recent years. The high court had been asked to review a pioneering program in Milwaukee, Wis., that allowed low-income children to transfer to private schools — including religious schools — at state expense. Opponents and supporters of school vouchers hoped the court would use the case to resolve a question that had long divided them: Can publicly funded voucher programs include religious schools without violating the constitutional separation of church and state?

In the end, neither side got the definitive ruling it wanted. The court announced Nov. 9 that it would not take up the case, letting stand a Wisconsin Supreme Court ruling the previous June that said Milwaukee's school-voucher plan did not violate the First Amendment's church-state separation clause.

Both opponents and supporters of school vouchers were disappointed by the court's action — or inaction, as some saw it — but each side put its own spin on the court's decision.

Voucher advocates claimed victory. If the Supreme Court justices had felt the Wisconsin program was clearly unconstitutional, they would have seized the opportunity to set the record straight, proponents said. "The Milwaukee decision was extremely strong and took a lot of wind out of opponents' sails," says Clint Bolick, litigation director for the libertarian-leaning Institute for Justice in Washington, D.C. "We're simply not hearing the constitutional argument as often as we were" prior to Nov. 9.

Meanwhile, admittedly disappointed opponents were quick to point out that the high court's refusal

From *The CQ Researcher,*
April 19, 1999.

to hear the case did not mean the justices felt the law passed constitutional muster. "It is nothing more than a decision not to decide," says Elliot M. Mincberg, legal director of People for the American Way, a group that promotes First Amendment rights. "They may be waiting for a better case to come along before they rule on it."

Yet Mincberg and other voucher opponents concede that some state legislators will interpret the court's silence as a green light to push for similar programs elsewhere. Five states are considering voucher legislation this spring (*see p. 103*), and supporters are optimistic that at least one of those bills — a ground-breaking program in Florida — will become law before the Legislature adjourns later this month. If it withstands likely court challenges, the Florida law would for the first time provide vouchers for all children, regardless of family income level, who are attending poorly performing public schools.

Supporters of school vouchers claim that public opinion is shifting in their direction, and a recent Gallup Poll appears to back them up. While half of the respondents to the 1998 survey opposed "allowing students and parents to choose a private school to attend at public expense," opposition was down sharply from 1993, when 74 percent were against

the idea. Over the same period, support for private-school choice rose from 24 to 44 percent. Support for government-funded vouchers was actually higher when the question was worded slightly differently. Fifty-one percent of those polled in 1998 favored "allowing parents to send their school-age children to any public, private or church-related school of their choice with the government paying all or part of the tuition." Two years earlier, 43 percent of those polled favored the idea while 54 percent opposed it. Opinion was evenly divided in the 1997 poll, which is done annually for the Phi Delta Kappa educational fraternity. [1] (*See poll results, p. 95.*)

Tax-funded vouchers are often discussed under the rubric of "school choice," a broader category that encompasses privately financed tuition-reimbursement programs, tuition tax credits and expansion of public charter schools, which are exempted from many bureaucratic restrictions so that they are freer to innovate.

Choice supporters claim their cause has gained momentum in recent years, pointing to the following developments:

• More than 50,000 low-income students in 40 cities will receive vouchers from private philanthropists and foundations next year. [2]

• Last September, Wall Street investor Ted Forstmann and Wal-Mart heir John Walton announced they were launching a $100 million Children's Scholarship Fund to give four-year scholarships to 40,000 low-income children in grades K–12 via a nationwide lottery. The winners will be announced on April 21.

• The number of charter schools operating in the U.S. has nearly tripled in the past two years, rising from 441 in 1996–97 to 1,207 in 1998-99. [3] (*See sidebar, p. 101.*)

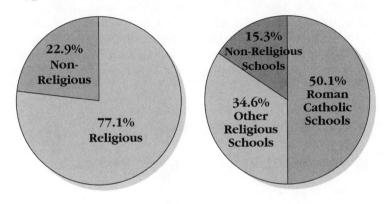

Most U.S. Private Schools Are Religious

More than three-quarters of the nation's private schools are religious; half of all private-school students attend Roman Catholic schools.

Types of Private Schools

- 22.9% Non-Religious
- 77.1% Religious

Students in Private Schools

- 15.3% Non-Religious Schools
- 34.6% Other Religious Schools
- 50.1% Roman Catholic Schools

Source: "Private School Universe Survey, 1995-96," National Center for Education Statistics, U.S. Department of Education, March 1998.

• The Arizona Supreme Court on Jan. 26 upheld a state law allowing up to $500 a year in tax-free donations to scholarship funds at private schools, including religious schools. Voucher advocates hope the decision will boost efforts to get publicly funded vouchers approved by the Arizona Legislature later this year.

Supporters say vouchers and other school-choice options are getting more attention because they make sense, especially to lower-income parents in urban areas. Without some type of economic aid, these parents often have no choice but to send their children to local public schools that are often overcrowded, poorly equipped and understaffed.

"The clear tide of public opinion is moving in favor of choice, even among African-Americans," says Michael Guerra, executive director of the National Catholic Education Association. Randy Tate, executive director of the Christian Coalition, agrees.

"As conservatives in Washington are grappling to find issues that resonate across ideological and political boundaries, school choice is one with broad-based appeal," he says.

Jim Carper, a specialist in the history of American education and an associate professor at the University of South Carolina at Columbia, detects a growing rift between the older black leadership of the 1960s, which he says "is committed to the public school system at any cost," and younger blacks who are open to discussing other educational options. "The desire for choice in education is very much alive and well in the African-American community," he says.

But while public support for school choice appears to be growing, it comes with strings attached. For instance, support for vouchers in the recent Gallup Poll was strongest if the government paid only part of the private school tuition tab. Only 48 percent favored subsidizing all the costs of private school tuition, while

52 percent favored partial compensation. And three-quarters of those polled believe any private school that accepts tax-funded vouchers should be held accountable to the state for how it spends the public's money, just as public schools are. And 70 percent say private schools that accept vouchers should be required to accept students from a broader range of ethnic and economic backgrounds and academic abilities than is now generally the case.

Many believe the question of accountability and concerns over admissions policies could well determine the outcome of the voucher debate. Private schools value their independence, and many vow not to accept voucher-supported students if the government interferes with their operations. Partly for that reason, opponents plan to fight state voucher legislation by trying to attach such requirements wherever voucher plans are proposed.

"If private schools are allowed to accept public money without being held accountable, the public is writing them a blank check," says Bob Chase, president of the National Education Association (NEA), the nation's largest teachers' union. "We would challenge any voucher program that does not have such requirements."

Chase disagrees with those who say the voucher movement is gaining momentum. Some supporters have become disenchanted with the concept, he says, because student academic performance has not improved as much as anticipated in districts with voucher programs. (*See story, p. 107.*) He also points out that voucher proposals were soundly defeated at the polls by voters in Oregon, California, Washington and Colorado over the last five years.

Sandra Feldman, president of the American Federation of Teachers, believes the momentum of the voucher movement will dissipate once the public understands the long-term impact. "It sounds terrific until you understand its Orwellian meaning: Give up on public education in America; stop investing in it, siphon off as much of its funding as you can to enable a few 'deserving poor' to go to private (mostly religious) schools and to hell with all the kids left behind," she wrote. [4]

The Clinton administration still staunchly opposes private school vouchers, although the president has indicated he would support charter schools and other programs offering greater choice within public schools. Private school vouchers "make my blood boil," Education Secretary Richard W. Riley told educators in Nashville last December. [5]

Gerald Tirozzi, then assistant secretary of Education for elementary and secondary education, said voucher programs are not the best solution to the problems facing public schools. For one thing, he pointed out, America's private schools can accommodate only about 6 million students. There are about 46 million children in public schools — a figure expected to reach 49 million by 2006.

A voucher system "can only accommodate a minimal number of public school students," Tirozzi wrote. "To think of vouchers as a credible solution to the problems of public education is to disregard most of America's students." [6]

Some opponents claim that school-choice advocates have a not-too-hidden agenda: While most of the focus to date has been on programs that would direct funds to low-income children and their parents, the critics say their ultimate goal is to make publicly funded vouchers available to all families, regardless of income.

Indeed, in Wisconsin some proponents want to do just that, threatening the fragile coalition of conservative Republicans and African-American leaders who crafted Milwaukee's original voucher program in the late 1980s. Currently those vouchers only go to families with incomes below 1.75 times the federal poverty level — about $28,000 for a family of four. Last August Milwaukee Mayor John Norquist shocked the black community when he said he favored eliminating the income cap and opening the program up to all students.

A teaching assistant brings a group of second-graders back from recess to Hope Tremont Academy, one of nearly 60 voucher schools in Cleveland, Ohio.

"I'll fight it," says Howard Fuller, the former superintendent of Milwaukee's schools and a staunch supporter of the current voucher program. Fuller, now director of the Institute for the Transformation of Learning at Marquette University, says "I don't support universal vouchers. I didn't get into this to get money for people who already have it."

"This is why most black groups like the NAACP are against vouchers," said Wisconsin state Rep. Annette Polly Williams, the author of the original voucher program. "Without the in-

come cap, choice just becomes a free-market program that keeps richer families happy and Catholic and Lutheran schools solvent with state money without any commitment to improve public schools." [7]

"It's significant that there's any support" for vouchers among blacks, [8] says Fuller, "since all of the so-called top African-American leadership has relentlessly bombarded the community with how negative this program is. Yet I believe African-American parents want the same kind of choices that people with money have in America."

Bolick of the Institute for Justice does not deny that the school-choice movement may have a broader agenda than getting economically disadvantaged children out of failing urban schools. "It remains to be seen whether the movement will ever make the jump to middle-income kids," he says. "That really depends on how bad the public schools get."

As state legislatures craft voucher bills this spring, here are some of the issues they are debating:

Will vouchers force public schools to improve?

Giving parents money that allows them to pull their children out of failing public schools and send them to private schools will inject competition into the educational system, voucher advocates say. Public schools would then have to improve or risk losing billions of dollars in federal, state and local funds allocated based on school enrollment numbers, they argue.

"Education should not be a monopoly," says Tate of the Christian Coalition. "But right now you have

Continued on p. 96

School Vouchers Are Gaining Support

The idea of giving government-funded vouchers to students who want to attend private schools is gaining support, according to a recent Gallup Poll, but support varies slightly depending on how the question is phrased.

1 *Should students be allowed to attend a private school at public expense?*

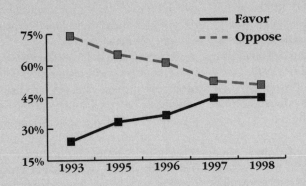

2 *Should parents be allowed to send their children to any public, private or church-related school of their choice with the government paying part or all of the tuition?*

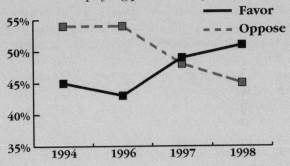

3 *Should government-issued vouchers cover all tuition costs, or just a portion of the costs?*

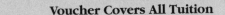

Voucher Covers All Tuition

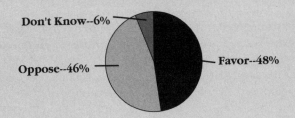

Don't Know--6%
Oppose--46%
Favor--48%

Voucher Covers Part of Tuition

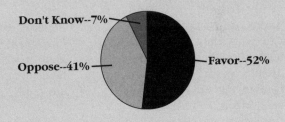

Don't Know--7%
Oppose--41%
Favor--52%

4 *Should private schools that accept government tuition payments be accountable to the state just like public schools are?*

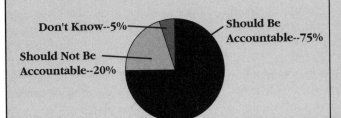

Don't Know--5%
Should Not Be Accountable--20%
Should Be Accountable--75%

5 *Should private schools that receive public funding be required to accept students from a wider range of backgrounds and academic abilities than is now generally the case?*

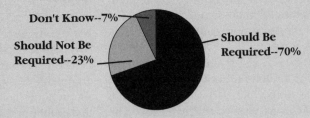

Don't Know--7%
Should Not Be Required--23%
Should Be Required--70%

Source: 1998 Phi Delta Kappa/Gallup Poll of the Public's Attitudes Toward the Public Schools

Continued from p. 94
Bill Clinton blocking the schoolhouse door, keeping children inside schools that don't work."

"I think the threat of vouchers has already helped to improve [public] education," says Joe McTigue, executive director of the Council for American Private Education. "And if the threat is enough to improve schools, imagine what the reality will do."

McTigue thinks the public's growing interest in vouchers is prompting the education establishment to support both education reform and public charter schools. Charter schools are small, tax-supported academies organized by parents, teachers or others in the community. They are freed from traditional regulations and red tape so they can focus on students' educational needs. (*See story, p. 101.*) "Charter schools are kind of a 'safe' form of school choice," McTigue says. "They are designed to give parents more choice within the public-school setting."

Public school teachers and administrators also are becoming more parent-friendly, McTigue says. "There's an effort to provide parents with what they want, and to treat them more like consumers," he says. "This is partly in response to the overhanging cloud of vouchers on the horizon."

Bolick agrees. As parents are given more educational choice, he says, the only way public schools can compete is by improving their product. "And that's exactly what we've seen in Milwaukee, where public schools all of a sudden are personalizing their programs, issuing guarantees of success, etc."

Fuller is more cautious than Bolick in assessing the impact of Milwaukee's voucher program on the city's public schools. Until this year, he points out, Milwaukee's voucher program was relatively small, with only about 1,000 participants. Now

that religious schools are eligible to participate, the program has expanded to 6,200 students.

Nevertheless, Fuller says, "We're beginning to see some signs of change. For the first time school administrators are running radio ads guaranteeing that they will teach your child how to read. For the first time in its 30-year history, the teachers' union and the administration reached a [contract] settlement six months before the old agreement expired. In that settlement, at least 12 schools began talking about seniority not being the basis for teacher staffing — something they said they would never do."

The NEA's Chase bristles at such talk. "I don't buy this education 'monopoly' language," he says. "Those are semi-inflammatory code words used by proponents of things other than vouchers."

Chase and other voucher opponents say there's no conclusive evidence that public schools improve because of private-school competition. Most of the improvements in student performance cited by voucher advocates can be attributed to the decades-old educational reform movement, Chase says. Voucher programs make those reforms more difficult to implement, he says. "How are public schools supposed to improve when they lose [financial] resources under voucher programs?" Chase asks.

"All this free-market talk really sounds good, but public schools are not widget factories," says NEA spokesman Stephen K. Wollmer. "They don't have control over their budgets the way a private company or a private school does. They can't borrow money and retool quickly if their product isn't selling."

The main flaw in the competition argument, Wollmer adds, is that private schools have much more latitude than public schools. "We don't have a level playing field," he says, noting

that private schools do not have to accept students with behavior problems or special education needs, who are more expensive to educate.

Mincberg at People for the American Way criticizes voucher programs — including the one in Milwaukee — that allow vouchers to go to students who already were enrolled in private schools. Mincberg's group has sued one such program in the Southeast Delco school district in suburban Philadelphia, which he says was set up "explicitly to benefit kids already enrolled in private Catholic schools."

Mincberg also believes the voucher movement is diverting attention from programs proven effective at raising student achievement. He points to the Student Achievement Guarantee in Education (SAGE) program in Wisconsin. Students in the two-year-old program — which provides smaller class sizes and after-school programs — improved their test scores in reading, math and language arts more than students in either the regular public schools or voucher schools. (*See story, p. 107.*)

Are voucher programs that include religious schools constitutional?

Milwaukee's school voucher program has been operating for nearly a decade. Initially, the city only allowed vouchers to be used to send students to non-religious private schools. In 1995, however, the Wisconsin Legislature voted to include religious schools in the program. But the expansion was put on hold after it was challenged in court.

On June 10, 1998, the Wisconsin Supreme Court ruled that incorporating religious schools into the program did not violate either the state or the U.S. Constitution. The court said the program's expansion was driven largely by a "secular purpose" — to expand educational opportunities for poor children. Additionally, the court

Private Schools Set Their Limits

Most private schools would be willing to accept students from overcrowded urban schools in exchange for tuition reimbursement if they could maintain their current policies regarding curriculum, admissions, student assessment and other issues, according to a 1997 survey by the U.S. Department of Education. But most religious schools would not participate if they had to allow transfer students to opt out of religious instruction, and only 31 percent of the private schools show some degree of willingness to participate if they were required to accept students with special needs such as learning disabilities, limited English proficiency or low achievement.

Percentage Willing to Participate in Voucher Programs Under Various Conditions

Condition	Definitely Willing	Probably Willing	Possibly Willing	Probably Unwilling	Definitely Unwilling
Maintain current policies	60%	17%	15%	4%	4%
Random assignment of transfer students	19%	17%	18%	18%	28%
Accept special-needs students	7%	8%	16%	27%	41%
Participate in state assessments	18%	15%	24%	15%	27%
Permit exemptions from religious instruction or activities	19%	6%	8%	9%	57%

Source: "Barriers, Benefits and Costs of Using Private Schools to Alleviate Overcrowding in Public Schools," Final Report, 1998, U.S. Department of Education. The study was based on data collected from 22 large urban areas with overcrowded public schools. Percentages may not total 100 because of rounding.

noted, any child attending a parochial school under the program could be excused from religious instruction if his or her parents requested such an exemption. [9]

The American Civil Liberties Union, People for the American Way and affiliates of the state's largest teachers' unions appealed the decision to the U.S. Supreme Court. Both supporters and opponents hoped a Supreme Court ruling would clarify what many view as a host of confusing and contradictory decisions on state support of religious schools.

While the Supreme Court had never ruled on the constitutionality of vouchers, it had looked at other schemes to help parents with educational expenses. In 1973, for example, the court ruled in *Committee for Public Education and Religious Liberty v. Nyquist* that a New York state law granting parents reimbursements and tax credits for private school tuition was unconstitutional. The court said the law had the effect of subsidizing religious education because roughly three-quarters of parents receiving the reimbursements or credits sent their children to church-related schools.

But over the next two decades, the court handed down several apparently contradictory rulings, including *Mueller v. Allen* in 1983. In that case, the court held that an Ohio law offering a parental tax deduction for tuition was constitutional even though 93 percent of those claiming the deduction had children in religious schools. [10]

The Supreme Court's 8-1 decision not to review the Wisconsin case was widely interpreted as a victory for supporters of school choice. The Supreme Court has left intact "the most definitive court decision [on the subject] to date, which solidly supports the constitutionality of school choice," Bolick told a reporter. [11] "The court's action clears the way for states to embark on further experiments with educational choice," says Mike McConnell, a law professor and constitutional scholar at the University of Utah.

That's just not true, insists the NEA's Chase. "Except in Wisconsin, the issue is still not settled. The court decided not to tackle the issue. I think the question will eventually have to go before the Supreme Court."

"A definitive ruling by the U.S.

Supreme Court is absolutely necessary," Bolick agrees.

In the meantime, the Supreme Court left the Wisconsin high court's ruling on the law intact. That court said the program was constitutional because the state was not directly funding religious institutions. Instead, the court noted, the money was given to parents, who then decided where to spend it. The Milwaukee program "merely adds religious schools to a range of pre-existing educational choices available to [Milwaukee] children," the court said.

The question of whether religious schools should be allowed to accept publicly funded tuition vouchers is critical to the school-choice movement. More than three-quarters of all private schools in the U.S. — and most of those in low-income neighborhoods — are church-affiliated. (*See graphs, p. 93.*) Proximity is not the only consideration for low-income families.

"The only schools most poor parents can afford — even with a voucher — are overwhelmingly religious," Mincberg says. The fact that vouchers tend to "push" poor students toward religious institutions makes them unconstitutional, he maintains.

McConnell at the University of Utah says that while the constitutionality of school vouchers is not resolved, using public funds to attend church-related institutions is a well-established practice at the preschool and college levels. "It has been clear for quite some time that the old argument that it is unconstitutional for any governmental money to be used by religious institutions . . . just flies in the face of consistent and relatively uncontroversial practices," he says.

For instance, college students receiving federal education grants and loans are free to attend state universities as well as religious schools ranging from Catholic Notre Dame to Mormon Brigham Young, he points

out. And families are free to use their federal child-care assistance to send their children to church-based day care, he says. "It just seems very peculiar to say that it's only between the first grade and 12th grade that the Constitution requires discrimination against religious institutions."

College and preschool education are "totally different animals than K-12," responds Chase, "because K-12 is compulsory. There's a big difference between someone being required to go to elementary and secondary school and someone choosing to go to college or to send their child to a day-care program."

Some proponents say voucher programs have a better chance of withstanding constitutional scrutiny if they include provisions allowing students to opt out of religious instruction — reasoning echoed by the Wisconsin Supreme Court ruling. But Mincberg disagrees. "It's not as if the only religion you get is in chapel every morning," he says. "Religion is embedded in the curriculums of church schools. That violates [Thomas] Jefferson's and [James] Madison's principle that not a farthing of compelled taxpayer dollars should go to support a religious point of view that [some] individuals disagree with."

Will vouchers hurt religious schools?

Some people fear that publicly funded tuition vouchers carry a hidden price tag: loss of independence.

"Government aid inevitably comes with strings attached," noted Howard P. Berkowitz, president of the Anti-Defamation League. [12]

"Private schools receiving vouchers ought to be held accountable for educating kids well, and should be subjected to the same performance and testing standards as public schools," says Mincberg. "They should also abide by [federal and state] civil rights laws and be fair in

their selection of students."

Some voucher programs specifically prohibit private schools from discriminating based on race, religion, ethnicity or disability in their admissions policies. Those voucher laws usually require that students be selected randomly.

"We've found that some schools have random selection on paper and then, in practice, they don't," Mincberg says. "They were giving preference to Catholic students or students in the parish. Up to one-third of voucher schools in Milwaukee may be in violation of random-selection requirements."

Chase is particularly concerned about private schools that limit the enrollment of students with special-education needs, such as learning disabilities, limited English proficiency or low achievement. "About 75 percent of private schools right now do not offer any kind of special-education service," Chase says. "We would challenge any voucher program that does not have such requirements" for participating schools.

Such demands for accountability could slow the voucher movement. "If voucher programs expose [religious] classrooms to new layers of government oversight, the choice movement could be dead on arrival," writes Joe Loconte, William E. Simon Fellow in Religion and a Free Society at the conservative Heritage Foundation. [13]

Most private schools appear willing to participate if they can maintain their current policies regarding curriculum, admissions, student assessment and the like. But a recent Department of Education survey found that many private schools would resist accepting randomly assigned voucher students. And most religious schools would not join a voucher program if publicly supported students could refrain from participating in religious instruction or religious activities. [14] (*See chart, p. 97.*)

"No religious school — certainly no Catholic school — is going to participate in any plan that asks the school to cease functioning as a religious institution," says Guerra at the National Catholic Education Association. "It makes no sense for them to do that."

While most Catholic schools in Milwaukee are participating in the city's voucher program, most Lutheran schools are not. "We feel it would compromise our mission as a Christian school," said John Wesenberg, principal of Garden Homes Lutheran School. [15]

John Holmes, director of government affairs for the Association of Christian Schools International, says his members would balk at a provision allowing students to opt out of religious activities. "If you choose to go to a religious school, then that option should include the whole package of what that school is about," he says. "Otherwise you're going to cut the heart out of the mission of the institution."

McTigue at the Council for American Private Education says voucher programs should be designed to minimize government interference. "If you regulate schools to the point where the difference between school A and school B is Tweedledee and Tweedledum, you've eliminated pluralism and the right of parents to select a school that best matches their child's needs," he says. ■

BACKGROUND

Movement's Origins

There is little that is genuinely new about school-choice plans. Maine's "tuitioning" program has existed since the 18th century, Vermont's since 1869.

Tuitioning programs are New England's version of vouchers. Small towns with no public high school pay the tuition for residents who attend approved public or private high schools located outside the town. In Vermont, students were allowed to attend religious schools until 1961, when a state Supreme Court ruling outlawed using government funds to pay tuition in parochial schools.

In 1994 the same court reversed itself and allowed tuition reimbursement for parents sending their children to sectarian schools. But the state's education commissioner continued to refuse to allow tuitioned students to be reimbursed for parochial school tuition. So the school board of tiny Chittenden, Vt., sued the state, arguing that based on the 1994 decision it should be allowed to send 15 town residents to a local Roman Catholic high school. The case has been appealed to the Vermont Supreme Court, where a decision is expected in June.

Observers say some of the arguments being used in the Vermont case hark back to xenophobic prejudices that permeated debate in the 1800s, when the nation's public education system was being established. In state after state, taxes were being levied to finance public education, and truancy laws were being passed to ensure compulsory attendance. But as education historian Carper points out, the noble goal of free education for all was promoted with often ignoble motives. [16]

"The history of American education is based on pernicious anti-Catholicism," Carper says. "In the 1830s to 1850s, waves of Roman Catholic immigration pushed a lot of Protestant Americans into a common educational front in favor of compulsory public education."

In Maine, "tuitioning" students were allowed to attend religious

schools until 1981, when the state disallowed the practice. But in 1997, the Institute for Justice sued Maine on behalf of parents from tuitioning towns who want to send their children to religious schools. The lawsuit argues that excluding religious schools violates constitutional guarantees of free exercise of religion and equal protection under the law.

After a lower court ruled against the parents, the case was appealed to the Maine Supreme Court, which heard oral arguments in November.

Voucher Proposals

While tuitioning programs have been around for centuries, most people trace the roots of the modern voucher movement to a seminal 1955 essay by free-market economist Milton Friedman. [17] He said vouchers would give parents greater flexibility in choosing their child's school, and would eventually improve public schools by injecting competition into the system. Vouchers would especially benefit the poor, he argued, because they often have no choice but to send their children to inferior local schools.

Eventually the federal government tested the voucher concept in a pilot program in elementary and junior high schools in the San Jose suburban school district of Alum Rock, Calif. The program ran from 1972 to 1976, but had lukewarm results, according to Denis P. Doyle, who ran the program. "It got a bad rap because it was not a startling success," said Doyle." [18]

In the early 1980s, the Reagan administration promoted a similar concept in the form of "tuition tax credits" for families with children at private and parochial schools. In 1990 the

Continued on p. 101

Chronology

1950s-1970s

The perception that public schools are inadequate gives birth to the school-choice movement.

1955
Libertarian economist Milton Friedman publishes an essay proposing tuition vouchers as a way of expanding educational opportunities and improving public schools.

June 25, 1973
U.S. Supreme Court rules in *Committee for Public Education and Religious Liberty v. Nyquist* that a New York state law giving parents reimbursements and tax credits for the cost of private tuition in religious schools is unconstitutional.

1980s *Concern about public education grows as student performance on the Scholastic Aptitude Test declines.*

June 29, 1983
Supreme Court upholds the constitutionality of a Minnesota law allowing parents to deduct part of their children's private or parochial school expenses from the family's taxable income in *Mueller v. Allen.*

1990s *The first school voucher pilot programs and charter schools are created.*

1990
In April the Wisconsin Legislature establishes the first school voucher pilot program, helping 1,100 low-income students in Milwaukee to pay tuition at private non-parochial schools.

1991
The Minnesota Legislature creates the first charter-school program. Indianapolis businessman J. Patrick Rooney creates the nation's first privately funded voucher program in Indianapolis. His action spurs dozens of similar programs in other cities around the country.

1994
The Vermont Supreme Court allows tuition reimbursements for parents sending their children to sectarian schools. The school board of tiny Chittenden later sues the state, arguing that based on this decision it should be allowed to send 15 town residents to a local Roman Catholic high school.

1995
In June the Ohio Legislature creates a pilot voucher program in Cleveland. Under the program, vouchers can be used in religious or non-religious schools. In July the Wisconsin Legislature expands the Milwaukee program to cover 15,000 students and allows the vouchers to be used at religious schools.

1996
In May an Ohio appellate court declares Cleveland's voucher plan unconstitutional, on the ground that it violates the separation of church and state clauses of both the state and federal constitutions. The case is appealed to the Ohio Supreme Court.

1997
In January a Wisconsin trial court rules that the state's law expanding the Milwaukee voucher program to include religious schools is unconstitutional. The Institute for Justice sues Maine on behalf of parents who want to send their children to religious schools. The lawsuit argues that excluding religious schools violates constitutional guarantees of free exercise of religion and equal protection under the law.

1998
In June, the Wisconsin Supreme Court rules in *Jackson v. Benson* that the Milwaukee voucher program is constitutional under both the state and U.S. constitutions. Opponents appeal the decision to the U.S. Supreme Court. On Nov. 9 the court refuses to review it. Congress passes a $7 million program to provide 2,000 children in Washington, D.C., with vouchers of up to $3,200 apiece, but President Clinton vetoes the legislation in July.

1999
On Jan. 14 New York City's Republican Mayor Rudolph W. Giuliani proposes establishing a Milwaukee-style pilot voucher program in one of the city's school districts. On March 25 the Florida House of Representatives votes 71-49 to give "opportunity scholarships" to students who attend schools that receive a failing grade two years in a row on new statewide achievement tests.

Are Charter Schools the Answer?

Unhappy with the education their children are getting in public schools, some parents are taking matters into their own hands. For a few, the solution is home schooling.[1] Others are finding the financial resources to send their children to private schools. And a growing number are taking advantage of laws in their states that allow parents, teachers or others in the community to operate "charter" schools within the public school system.

These small, innovative academies are generally freed from many curriculum requirements and from such constraints as local teacher salary scales and collective-bargaining agreements. They are free to hire their own teachers and experiment with new teaching techniques. The idea is to relieve schools of bureaucratic burdens so that they can focus on students' educational needs.

"The [charter-school] movement was founded on the premise that when you eliminate red tape and give the principal decision-making power and encourage parents' input, that's an equation for success," says Joe McTigue, executive director of the Council for American Private Education.

Advocates believe competition from charter schools will stimulate public schools to be more innovative and more responsive to parents' concerns. "Competition from charter schools is the best way to motivate the ossified bureaucracies governing too many public schools," Sen. Joseph Lieberman, D.-Conn., wrote recently.[2]

Since the early 1990s, 33 states and the District of Columbia have passed legislation authorizing charter schools. More than 1,200 charter schools are in operation nationwide, and another 200 have been approved to open

next year.

Many charter schools target students at-risk of falling through the cracks in traditional public schools. For instance, the Apple School in Lakeland, Fla., serves more than 100 children diagnosed with Attention Deficit Hyperactivity Disorder (ADHD). "Most charter schools target a specific population of kids," says Lakeland's administrator, Roy Williams.

Charter schools have drawn fire from some in the public school community. Bob Chase, president of the National Education Association, says he supports the charter-school concept but opposes "permissive" laws that "grant charter status not just to legitimate public schools but also to existing private schools, to home-schoolers and even to individuals and for-profit companies with no track record whatsoever in education." The charter-school movement is being used to get "backdoor funding for schools that remain effectively private by relabeling them 'charters,'" Chase says.[3]

The Center for Education Reform, which tracks and assesses charter-school laws in the states, insists the only way such schools can succeed is if the laws authorizing them contain few restrictions. This is the only way to guarantee that charter schools won't be regulated to death, the group says. "Yet today," the center notes in its latest report, "some charter-school laws are voluminous, reflecting the growing alarm felt by many in traditional public education venues toward this new form of public school."[4]

The center's report also criticizes communities for imposing new restrictions on charter schools. It points to Tucson, Ariz., as an example. "Having failed to ward off

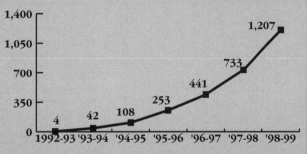

Number of Charter Schools Rose Quickly

The number of charter schools operating in the United States has nearly tripled in the past two years.

Source: The Center for Education Reform, "National Charter School Directory 1998-1999"

Continued from p. 99

Brookings Institution published a book by voucher advocates Terry M. Moe and John E. Chubb calling for a radical restructuring of American education. They recommended that public, private and religious schools compete for students in a free market.[19]

Then in the late 1980s, Polly Williams, an African-American state rep-resentative, took up the school-choice banner in Wisconsin. Arguing that black parents were tired of having their children bused to outlying schools to achieve racial balance, she called for drastic action to improve neighborhood schools and proposed Milwaukee's voucher pilot program.

When it began in 1990, Milwaukee's program authorized $2,446 apiece for up to 1,100 low-income students to attend non-religious schools. The first year only 337 students participated because there were not enough private school spaces available. Enrollment jumped to 5,830 this academic year — from 1,501 last year — mainly because inner-city Catholic schools are now eligible to accept voucher students.

Proponents Worry That Regulations Will Limit Success

charters in their city, the [Tucson] City Council amended municipal zoning requirements to prohibit the opening of any new charter school not located on at least five acres or not having approved traffic patterns in place," the report says.

It's a common practice, notes Tracy Bailey, who oversees Florida's charter schools. "We call it regulatory reloading." [5]

There have been no nationwide studies to date that evaluate whether charter schools are more effective at educating students than traditional public schools. "It is still too early for a comprehensive report on the impact of charter schools, but so far results are encouraging," Lieberman wrote. He citied studies in Massachusetts and Minnesota showing students in charter schools surpassing state academic standards.

The Center for Education Reform's recent report also offers anecdotal evidence of charter schools' success, including test scores from students at two charter schools in California — Horizon Instructional Systems in Lincoln and the Vaughn Next Century Learning Center in San Fernando — that far exceeded district averages.

Arizona has 311 charter schools, more than any other state; 6 percent of Arizona's public school students are enrolled in charter schools this year. But a recent state evaluation found that students in charter schools "are not performing very differently from [students in] regular public schools." In math, students in traditional public schools showed gains equivalent to students in charter schools. By middle school, students attending charter schools for one or more years lagged behind students in regular schools, and the lag widened among high school students.

Lisa Graham Keegan, Arizona's superintendent of public instruction and an outspoken advocate of charter schools, puts a positive spin on the findings. The lags in achievement may be attributed to the fact that many charter schools focus on potential dropouts or other students who are failing in regular schools, she says.

Those students "tend to start at a lower point," said Rob Melnick, director of the Morrison Institute for Public Policy, which conducted the study. [6]

The study did offer clues about why charter schools are so popular: 79 percent of Arizona parents with children in charter schools felt their children were performing better academically, and 77 percent said their children had better attitudes about learning. Eighty-three percent of students in charter schools said they were doing better than at their previous school, while 77 percent liked their teachers better. [7]

NEA's Chase remains cautious. "I think there may be some merit in charter schools," he says. "My concern is that there is no silver bullet to improving schools. Yet there is this headlong rush into charter schools, especially in states like Arizona."

Chase says it is unfair for the states and federal government to pass legislation demanding increased accountability and improved test scores from the public schools — and basing teacher tenure and employment on those results — while exempting charter schools and private schools from those same requirements.

"People say the reason we need charter schools is that there is less regulation," he complains. "But you have legislatures that pass charter-school legislation today and then pass legislation increasing the amount of regulation of public schools."

"If public schools are overregulated, then why do they keep regulating them?" he asks.

---

[1] For background, see Charles S. Clark, "Home Schooling," *The CQ Researcher*, Sept. 9, 1994, pp. 769-792.

[2] Joseph Lieberman, "Schools Where Kids Succeed," *Reader's Digest*, January 1999.

[3] Bob Chase, "Avoid Pitfalls in Charter School Law," *The [Memphis] Commercial Appeal*, March 28, 1999.

[4] "Charter School Laws: State by State Ranking and Profiles," The Center for Education Reform, November 1998.

[5] Quoted on "Charter Schools, Part I," *Morning Edition*, National Public Radio, Nov. 3, 1997.

[6] Quoted in Paul Davenport, "Study says charter students' gains similar to others," The Associated Press, March 15, 1999.

[7] *Ibid.*

But enrollment is still nowhere near the 15,000 students authorized by the state Legislature in 1995.

Since the program's inception the amount paid for each voucher has increased every year, reaching $4,894 in 1998-99. The total amount of educational funds shifted from Milwaukee public schools to private schools because of vouchers rose from $733,000 in 1990-91, the program's first year of operation, to $7 million in 1997-98. The amount of money lost by public schools rose sharply in 1998-99, to $28 million, after religious schools began participating in the program. [20]

Ohio was the first state to enact a law allowing religious schools to participate in a voucher program.

Under Cleveland's 1995 pilot voucher program, 2,000 elementary school students were eligible to receive up to $2,500 to attend the private school of their choice. Although the law was the first to allow all students to receive vouchers, it stipulates that preference should be given to low-income students. The constitutionality of that law has been challenged, however, and is awaiting a ruling by the Ohio Supreme Court.

War in Milwaukee

In Milwaukee, the controversy over school vouchers remains as heated as ever. Teachers' unions, civil rights activists and anti-voucher groups are refusing to back down, despite the Supreme Court's refusal to review the law.

"It's like a war in Milwaukee," says former school Superintendent Fuller. "It's an issue that divides people politically, philosophically and ideologically. Now that the legal battle is over, [opponents] are going to try to regulate the program to death."

Judith Schaeffer, deputy legal director for People for the American Way, explains the group's position: "We believe strongly that if the program is to proceed, it must proceed lawfully. It's very clear that the regulations are being violated."

When the Wisconsin Legislature expanded the voucher program in 1995, it required participating schools to admit students by random selection and to allow students to opt out of religious instruction — two restrictions that in practice may discourage private schools from participating and give opponents additional ammunition to challenge such programs.

In fact, the People for the American Way Foundation (PFAWF) and the Milwaukee chapter of the NAACP filed a complaint with the state on Feb. 2 claiming that more than a third of the participating private schools may be violating the random-admissions requirement by giving preferential admissions to Catholics and siblings of current students.

"The voucher program was sold to Wisconsin legislators, and indeed defended before the Wisconsin Supreme Court, with the promise that all voucher students would get an equal chance to participate through random selection, not selection based on religious belief or other factors," says legal director Mincberg. "That promise has been broken."

"This new evidence that voucher schools are not obeying the law reinforces our strong belief that vouchers are the wrong choice for Milwaukee and throughout the United States," said PFAWF President Carole Shields. "We will continue to work with the NAACP and other concerned groups in Milwaukee to make sure that vouchers are not being used to open the door to new discrimination against schoolchildren there — and to oppose such programs around the country," she said. [21]

Milwaukee has clearly become ground zero in the public relations battle for hearts and minds in the voucher debate, Fuller says. "Anti-choice forces are doing everything they can to create the worst type of political and public relations environment imaginable." Vouchers have become a hot political issue in the city as well. "Money is pouring in for both sides in the current school board election in amounts I've never seen before," Fuller says.

Fuller's group recently held a symposium that brought together 200 African-Americans from around the country to study how to use school-choice options like vouchers, charter schools and tax credits. "We've got to figure out how to use these things to benefit our children," he says.

Carper at the University of South Carolina says African-Americans are more open to the idea of non-public education than they were in the 1960s. "Thirty years ago you wouldn't have found an African-American leader who would have even entertained the notion of vouchers or would have spoken of non-public education at all positively," he says, "and with good reason. A lot of non-

public education frankly had racist baggage attached to it."

But private education is different now, he says. "I sit on a Christian school board here in Columbia, and we have one of the most racially and ethnically cosmopolitan schools in the state. It's a different world." ■

CURRENT SITUATION

Action in the States

After a decade of debate, there still are no statewide programs that permit parents to send their children to private schools at public expense. But proposals for pilot voucher programs and broader educational reforms are being debated across the country, particularly in states with Republican governors and conservative legislatures. "The states have become laboratories of school-choice experimentation," Bolick says.

Legislators in at least five states are considering voucher legislation this year: Florida, Texas, New Mexico, Pennsylvania and Arizona. New York City Mayor Rudolph W. Giuliani has proposed establishing a Milwaukee-style voucher system as a pilot program in one of the city's 32 community school districts.

In Florida, tuition vouchers are part of a broader education-reform package championed by newly elected Republican Gov. Jeb Bush, son of former President George Bush. Under the plan, Florida schools would be graded according to student performance on statewide achievement tests, which are already given to students in grades 4, 5, 8 and

10. Under the governor's plan, those tests would be given annually in grades 3-10. Students who attend schools that receive a "failing" grade two years in a row would become eligible for state-funded "opportunity scholarships" that could be used to attend the public or private schools of their choice. Schools receiving the highest grades would be eligible for additional state funds, which could be used as they see fit.

The vouchers would not be restricted to low-income families, but proponents argue that the principal beneficiaries are likely to be children from poorer neighborhoods. "If the schools are that bad, the middle- and upper-income kids will have fled," Bolick says.

The bill, which overwhelmingly passed the Florida House March 25 by a 71-49 vote, now goes before the state Senate, which is expected to take it up before the legislative session ends this month.

Critics of the Florida proposal say it does not include specific provisions holding private schools accountable for how they spend the public's money. Indeed, opponents tried to attach more than 80 amendments to the bill aimed at requiring private schools receiving state funds to be accountable. Among other things, the provisions would have required participating schools to administer the same statewide achievement tests that public school students must take, to undergo state financial audits and to abide by the same non-discrimination admission standards as public schools. All of the amendments were rejected by the Republican-controlled House.

"I am floored by the potential for waste, fraud and fiscal irresponsibility in this bill — and by the idea that we can fix our public schools by abandoning them," said Lisa Versaci, Florida director of People for the American Way. [22] Her group claims the proposed law would violate both the U.S. and Florida constitutions and has vowed to challenge it in court.

Nonetheless, supporters are confident the bill will pass. Vouchers were hotly debated during last year's governor's race and were strongly supported by then-candidate Bush. "Of all the states, I would put the odds very high for Florida to pass legislation this year," says Bolick.

In Texas, Gov. George W. Bush, a likely Republican presidential candidate, is supporting a bill that would extend school choice to low-income, low-performing youngsters in the state's six largest cities: Houston, Dallas, San Antonio, Ft. Worth, Austin and El Paso. Under the plan, which passed the Senate education committee March 24, students would receive vouchers worth 80 percent of the per-pupil funds allocated by the state and local school district; no more than 5 percent of a district's students could receive vouchers. Preference would be given to students at risk of dropping out of school.

It is unclear at this point whether the bill has the support of two-thirds of the Republican-controlled Senate, which it would need to be debated on the floor. It faces an even tougher challenge in the Democrat-controlled House, supporters say.

In Pennsylvania, Republican Gov. Tom Ridge unveiled a plan on March 11 to provide "supervouchers" worth $2,000-$4,000 a year to students attending schools classified as "academically distressed." The program would be limited to eight primarily urban school districts, which also would be granted broad powers to institute educational reform.

Earlier, Ridge proposed a groundbreaking pilot program that, if enacted, would allow families earning up to $75,000 a year to qualify for private-school vouchers. The money for the "middle-class" vouchers would not come from state education funds, however. Instead the state would appropriate $587.2 million in new money over five years. The proposed program was suggested by Catholic school officials in Pennsylvania as a means of reducing overcrowding in the public schools. Most of the 15 school districts selected for the program have a large number of Catholic schools. Bolick says the proposal emerged as a compromise between minority legislators, who pushed for the supervoucher plan, and Republicans, who lobbied for the statewide pilot program.

Arizona has more school choice than any other state in the country. There is complete open enrollment across district lines. The state also has the largest number of charter schools in the United States — 311, according to state Superintendent of Public Instruction Lisa Graham Keegan — and allows tax credits for private school scholarships, the plan recently legitimized by the Arizona Supreme Court.

Last July, Arizona enacted a pioneering school-financing plan called "student-centered education funding." Under the new law, which applies only to public schools, the state assigns each student the amount of per-pupil money spent by the state each year on non-capital expenses. When the student enrolls in the school of his choice — either a charter school or a regular public school — the state then releases the money to that institution.

"We used to finance education based on property taxes, like most of America," Keegan says. "Wealthier neighborhoods naturally got more money than lower-income neighborhoods, even though they were paying taxes at the same rate. It cannot be overstated enough how inherently unequal those systems are."

Now Keegan and Republican Gov. Jane Dee Hull are championing a statewide, Milwaukee-style voucher program that would provide about $4,800 a year for low-income students to use in any school of their choice, including religious schools. The measure passed the Arizona House March 15 and is now being considered in the state Senate.

In New Mexico, Republican Gov. Gary E. Johnson is committed to enacting some sort of school voucher program, but he faces a heavily Democratic legislature. Johnson recently proposed a precedent-setting voucher program, which would have phased in the first statewide, universal voucher program in the country. Beginning with low-income students the first year, the program would have eventually provided vouchers to all 330,000 students in the state, regardless of family income, by the end of the fourth year.

When the legislature refused to enact his proposal, Johnson threatened to veto the state budget, effectively shutting down the state government, unless the Legislature at least approved a pilot program for school vouchers. Because the legislative session ended without a budget, the governor is expected to convene a special legislative session before the fiscal year ends on June 30. [23] ■

OUTLOOK

Universal Vouchers?

O pponents say vouchers for low-income students are the nose of the camel peaking under the tent, paving the way for universal vouchers. They cite the voucher programs proposed this year in Florida, Pennsylvania and New Mexico, which do not specifically limit vouchers to low-income families.

"Without specific income caps, such programs could easily be expanded at a later date to become universal voucher programs," says Mincberg. Programs like the one being considered in Florida — which would give vouchers to any student in a low-achieving school — would be particularly easy to expand by simply using the laudable goal of raising state achievement standards, he argues.

"Ironically, as states increase the academic standards public schools must meet, the effect would be to make more and more students eligible for vouchers," Mincberg says, "without giving those schools the opportunity to improve before the kids start leaving. You wind up draining money and kids from those schools instead of focusing efforts on improving the schools."

Fuller says opponents are using the specter of universal vouchers as a scare tactic. "Clearly there are people who support universal vouchers, but I don't know of any nationwide effort to do that," he says.

Even in Milwaukee, where Mayor Norquist has come out in support of universal vouchers, the idea has never been officially proposed, Fuller points out. "Our coalition — which includes the mayor — has never united around universal vouchers, nor will we," he says. "There are too many people like myself who oppose them."

Tate of the Christian Coalition doesn't hide his support for universal vouchers. "I've said throughout the debate that if we want everyone to have an opportunity to achieve the American dream, every family should be able to send their children to a safe, secure and academically challenging school," he says. "But we need to start where the problem is most severe — in the inner cities where kids attend schools that most Americans don't want to drive past, let alone drop their children off at."

Bolick acknowledges that it could be difficult to stop the expansion of vouchers to other demographic groups. Once you have more school choice, he says, "it's not going to shrink. It's likely to grow, as more and more people demand the benefits. Whether it will make that jump to a universal choice plan, I just don't know."

Proponents predict that as more states embrace vouchers, more private schools will open up to fill the demand. "When the dollars are there, the market will open up and capacity will expand," says McTigue. "Black and Hispanic churches will establish schools in the inner cities. The private sector will respond, and educators fed up with the red tape in the public system will create new schools."

Many new private and charter schools have already opened up in Milwaukee. "The entire marketplace is in flux," says Bolick. "Who knows? Maybe one day we'll see movement back into improved Milwaukee public schools. That will be a sign that the program is succeeding."

Opponents remain skeptical. "Widespread use of vouchers will seriously undermine public education," Mincberg says. "The negative effect of vouchers will far outweigh any possible positive effects, due to the millions of dollars that will be drained away from the public school system."

And, Mincberg says, there is no guarantee that all this increased choice will actually result in better-educated children. "These voucher programs require no accountability," he says. "So you could be moving from a public school to a private school that is just as bad."

Others fear widespread use of vouchers could lead to a Balkanization of society and increased intolerance among future generations. "Public schools are the only institutions in our society where

Continued on p. 107

At Issue:

Are voucher programs that include church-related schools constitutional?

CLINT BOLICK
Litigation Director, Institute for Justice, Washington, D.C.

WRITTEN FOR *THE CQ RESEARCHER*, JULY 10, 1998

*t*he Wisconsin Supreme Court answered the constitutionality question with a resounding "yes" last year. The question will linger until the U.S. Supreme Court delivers a definitive decision. But the First Amendment's plain meaning, buttressed by an unbroken line of recent U.S. Supreme Court precedents, suggests that well-crafted school-choice programs will survive constitutional scrutiny.

The actual First Amendment language reads: "Congress shall make no law respecting an establishment of religion." Clearly, the framers meant only to proscribe direct sponsorship of religion, a conclusion buttressed by constitutional history.

Moreover, the First Amendment guarantees citizens the right to "free exercise" of religion. When the two religion clauses are read together, it is clear that the First Amendment directs the state to chart a neutral course.

The strongest (and really only) precedent in the opponents' arsenal is the U.S. Supreme Court decision in *Committee for Public Education and Religious Liberty v. Nyquist*. The 1973 decision invalidated a New York "parochaid" program that provided tax benefits and direct subsidies for private education, most of which went to religious schools. The court reasoned that the aid had the impermissible "primary effect" of advancing religion. The court expressly left open the question of "a case involving some sort of public assistance (for example, scholarships) made available generally without regard to the sectarian-nonsectarian, or public-nonpublic nature of the institution benefited."

Two things have changed in the years since *Nyquist*. First, the nature of school choice: It is no longer designed to benefit particular schools but rather is a remedial effort to help expand the range of educational options. Second, the Supreme Court itself has changed: As the court observed only last year, First Amendment jurisprudence has "significantly changed" over the past decade, specifically "our understanding of the criteria used to assess whether aid to religion has an impermissible effect."

Allowing private- and religious-school options not only accords with First Amendment principles but also with the deeply entrenched constitutional principles of parental sovereignty and equal educational opportunities. Forty-five years ago in *Brown v. Board of Education*, the U.S. Supreme Court promised equal educational opportunities for all children. Upholding the constitutionality of school choice will be a major step toward fulfilling that promise.

ELLIOT M. MINCBERG
Legal Director, People for the American Way

WRITTEN FOR *THE CQ RESEARCHER*, MARCH 1999

*d*espite persistent assertions by the Religious Right to the effect that a Wisconsin law expanding vouchers to include religious schools was held constitutional by the U.S. Supreme Court, the court refused to hear the case — issuing no ruling on the merits one way or the other.

Instead, it chose to let the Wisconsin law stand for the time being, subject to future rulings of the court.

The truth is that voucher programs that include sectarian schools grossly violate the constitutional separation of church and state. It is not simply that such schools might require students to engage in worship of other religious practices that violate their own or their parents' beliefs. It is that religion is in most sectarian schools entirely inseparable from academics.

According to the federal National Center for Education Statistics, more than half of all Christian schools describe "religious development," not academic excellence, as their top priority. Accordingly, faith is woven into the curriculum. In science class, for example, Christian schools are far more likely to ignore evolution in favor of Creationism. Sex-education classes are more likely to tailor instruction on birth control and disease prevention to their own religious doctrine or omit it altogether.

In short, voucher programs that fund religious instruction are unconstitutional because a primary effect is to advance religion. Quite simply, the majority of children participating in such voucher programs receive religious instruction paid for by taxpayers. That instruction will not just be in the form of worship services; it will be integrated into the curriculum from morning homeroom to biology, to literature to health, to after-school clubs and activities. Indeed, in Wisconsin, the law seems to permit schools to compel participation in religious worship over the objections of the student, or in the absence of written instructions from a parent.

Religious schools are created to advance a religious mission. That mission is perfectly reasonable and appropriate. But it may not be supported with tax dollars.

The Supreme Court ruled vouchers unconstitiutional in *Nyquist* in 1973, and will eventually break its silence on the current generation of voucher proposals. And when it does, it should stand by its previous rulings and strike down taxpayer financing of religious instruction, or it will ignore decades of settled constitutional law and key constitutional principles protecting religious liberty.

Do Students in Voucher Programs ...

For years, educators have been trying to determine whether students who use vouchers to attend private schools do better than those who remain in public school.

Not surprisingly, voucher opponents and proponents both say that their studies "prove" their position in the voucher debate. But no sooner has the ink dried on one study than the opposing side alleges bias and "bad social science."

"The right wing has conducted a profoundly deceptive public relations campaign seeking to persuade the media that these programs have been far more successful" than they have been, says People for the American Way, which opposes vouchers. In fact, "Some voucher students have done marginally better, some have done no better and some have fallen behind." [1]

"There are anecdotal instances that kids do better, and parents are more likely to be happy when they have chosen voucher programs," says Elliot M. Mincberg, the group's legal director. "But in terms of actual educational performance, I have not seen evidence that vouchers improve learning in any substantial way."

State-commissioned evaluations of the nation's two publicly funded voucher programs, in Milwaukee and Cleveland, showed no appreciable academic gains. Harvard University Professor Paul E. Peterson, a leading supporter of vouchers, has challenged both reports. In turn, the methodology and objectivity of Peterson and his colleagues have been widely challenged by researchers.

In a 1997 evaluation of Milwaukee's program, University of Wisconsin political science Professor John F. Witte found that voucher students did no better in reading compared with those who applied to the program but were rejected. But the voucher students performed better in math in the third and fourth years of the program. However, because half of the control-group students left the public school system and many of the least successful voucher students dropped out of the program, the findings were extremely "fragile," Witte said. [2]

After Witte reported his findings, voucher supporters lobbied successfully to eliminate the state requirement that participating schools gather achievement data necessary for a rigorous annual evaluation, Mincberg says.

Peterson says of the Witte report: "an acrid stench surrounds the manner in which the evaluator was selected." Peterson points out that Witte was chosen by Superintendent of Public Instruction Herbert Grover, "no friend of school choice." "Instead of putting up the evaluation for competitive bid," Peterson writes, "he gave the assignment to John Witte," who "was known to have doubts about the advantages of private education." [3]

Peterson's study of the Milwaukee program found that math scores for third- and fourth-year participants were 5 and 11 percent higher, respectively, than the scores of voucher applicants who weren't chosen and remained in public schools. Reading scores for students who had been in the voucher program for three and four years averaged 3 and 6 percent higher, respectively, he found. Peterson claimed that if similar success could be achieved for all minority students nationwide, it could close the gap between white and minority test scores by more than one-half. [4]

But voucher opponents vehemently attacked Peterson's findings as methodologically flawed. Most concluded that he and his colleagues had compared a small, select group of voucher students with a tiny and disproportionately disadvantaged group of public school students, biasing results in favor of the voucher students. Because of high attrition rates among both sample groups, by the fourth year the two groups were "about as similar as apples and nails," said an American Federation of Teachers (AFT) analysis of the Peterson study. [5]

In a 1996 paper, Peterson and a colleague answered criticisms of their Milwaukee study. Among other things, they said that the claim that missing cases contaminate the results "is not supported by a detailed look at the available evidence." They also contended that the "assertion that the number of cases is too small to warrant the inferences [we] draw is unsupported." [6]

The AFT further complained that Peterson's study did not adequately compensate for the differing education levels of the students' parents. In a later analysis, when Peterson did control for parent education, he said he

Continued from p. 105

people of all races and ethnic backgrounds learn to live together," says the NEA's Chase.

McTigue calls the Balkanization argument a "red herring." Private school graduates "are no less committed to democratic principles, pluralism and tolerance than gradu-ates of other schools," he says, citing research by Jay P. Greene, an assistant professor at the University of Texas at Austin. Greene found that private schools are more racially integrated than public schools. [24]

The Balkanization argument "raises my blood pressure," Guerra says. Religious schools bring a vision to education entirely consistent with democratic ideals, he argues. Religious education promotes the common good of the community, "and not just individual advancement or corporate economic growth," he says.

... Outperform Students in Public Schools?

found no significant difference in achievement between voucher students and their public school peers.

A study by Princeton University Professor Cecilia Rouse found no improvement in reading but substantial improvement in math among voucher students in Milwaukee. Voucher proponents and opponents both claimed Rouse's findings buttressed their arguments. [7]

In another study, Rouse found that students in Milwaukee's experimental Student Achievement Guarantee in Education (SAGE) program, featuring public schools with small classes, keep pace with voucher schools in math and substantially outpace both private schools and city magnet schools in reading. [8]

Similarly, Professor Alex Molnar of the University of Wisconsin-Milwaukee also found that reducing class size is more effective than voucher policy in helping at-risk students. Molnar also studied SAGE students and found they outperform students who attend public or private schools with larger class sizes. Molnar found that African-American males particularly benefit from SAGE's smaller class sizes. Total reading, language arts and math scores for black males in the smaller classes rose 56 points in one year, compared with 39.4 points in non-SAGE schools. [9]

Nevertheless, Mincberg complains, Gov. Tommy G. Thompson, R-Wis., has proposed a budget for next year that would fund SAGE programs in only 40 percent of Milwaukee's schools, compared with 70 percent of eligible schools outside the city.

Peterson says he expects to get more conclusive results from his study of the School Choice Scholarship Foundation program in New York City. The privately funded program awarded 1,200 low-income students $1,400 a year to attend the religious or secular school of their choice. Because the recipients were selected via a lottery from among 20,000 applicants, Peterson says he is confident his comparison of the performance of voucher students and those not selected will be more credible than earlier studies, since they all came from the same pool of students.

Preliminary results after one year show that voucher students in the fourth and fifth grades scored 4 percentage points higher in reading and 6 points higher in math than their public school peers. However, in comparing all students in grades two through five, the voucher students scored 2 points higher in both subjects.

"The results from the first year of the New York City evaluation suggest that ... there are clear benefits for low-income minority students that come from attendance in private schools," wrote Peterson. [10]

"There are dueling studies all over the place," concludes Clint Bolick, litigation director for the pro-voucher Institute for Justice in Washington, D.C. "But we should not give undue emphasis to the social scientists, who will undoubtedly continue to slug this out. The real experts are not the social scientists but the parents, who are voting with their feet."

---

[1] People for the American Way Foundation, "Myths and Facts about School Vouchers," undated Editorial Memorandum.

[2] John F. Witte, "Achievement Effects of the Milwaukee Voucher Program," Department of Political Science, Robert La Follette Institute, University of Wisconsin-Madison, Feb. 7, 1997.

[3] Paul E. Peterson and Chad Noyes, "Under Extreme Duress, School Choice Success," February 1996, chapter prepared for Diane Ravitch and Joseph Viteritti, eds, *New Schools for a New Century: The Redesign of Urban Education.*

[4] Jay P. Greene, Paul E. Peterson and Jiangtao Du, "Effectiveness of School Choice: The Milwaukee Experiment," March 1997.

[5] "A Critical Analysis of the Greene-Peterson-Du Paper," American Federation of Teachers Web site, September 1996, www.aft.org/research/reports/private/gdp/aftresp.htm.

[6] Jay P. Greene and Paul E. Peterson, "Methodological Issue in Evaluation Research: The Milwaukee School Choice Plan," Program on Education Policy and Governance, Harvard University, Aug. 29, 1996. Peterson is director of the program.

[7] Cecilia Rouse, "Private School Vouchers and Student Achievement: An Evaluation of the Milwaukee Parental Choice Program," *The Quarterly Journal of Economics,* Vol. 113, No. 2, 1998.

[8] Cecilia Rouse, "Schools and Student Achievement; More Evidence from the Milwaukee Public Choice Program," *Economic Policy Review,* 1998.

[9] Alex Molnar, "Smaller Classes, Not Vouchers, Increase Student Achievement," Keystone Research Center, 1998.

[10] Paul E. Peterson, "Vouchers and Test Scores," *Policy Review,* January-February 1999.

More Reforms

The public school system in the United States "can't possibly look the same in 10 years," say Arizona's Keegan. "It needs to be a better, more competitive mix of traditional pub-

lic, charter and private schools."

Some think tuition tax credits and tax-free education accounts will become more popular than vouchers, because they are less likely to provoke government meddling. Congress last year passed a bill allowing parents to set aside as much as $2,000

a year per child into tax-free "education savings accounts" that could be used for private school tuition. President Clinton vetoed the bill last July, but it has been reintroduced this year. Idaho and Virginia are also considering tuition tax credit bills this spring, and citizens in Michigan and California are seeking referendums on tax credits in 2000.

The number of home-schooled students also is likely to grow, partly because of the growing variety of distance-learning programs available through technology.[25] "The traditional concept of school will change dramatically," McTigue predicts.

Mincberg foresees more standards-based, results-oriented public school reforms. "I think we will also see a greater push to reduce class size, particularly in the younger grades," he says. "And we'll see more teachers being hired and more school construction going on, as well as a greater commitment to resources dedicated to public schools, particularly in urban areas."

"We will no longer be throwing dollar bills at schools without structural change first," predicts Tate. "Schools not doing their job will be forced to do a better job. You will see a marked increase in test scores because more children will be in schools that challenge them."

Schools will be more responsive to the needs of children and families," says McTigue. "Monopolies are notoriously insensitive to the needs of their clients. But when you have the ability to take your business someplace else, the market becomes responsive to your needs.

"The key is to shift power from the bureaucrats to the families and parents," McTigue says. "Once the consumer gets control of this thing, everybody's boat is going to rise. It will be good for public education, private schools, home schools — the whole shebang." ∎

Notes

[1] See Lowell C. Rose and Alec M. Gallup, "Public's Attitudes Toward the Public Schools," *Phi Delta Kappan*, September 1998.

FOR MORE INFORMATION

Council for American Private Education, PMB 457, 13017 Wisteria Dr., Germantown, Md. 20874; (301) 916-8460, www.capenet.org. This coalition of private-school associations seeks greater access to private schools for all Americans.

Institute for Justice, 1717 Pennsylvania Ave. N.W., #200, Washington, D.C. 20006; (202) 955-1300, www.instituteforjustice.org. This conservative public-interest law firm litigates cases involving parental school choice.

National Education Association, 1201 16th St. N.W., Washington, D.C. 20036; (202) 833-4000, www.nea.org. The NEA is the nation's largest teachers' union, with more than 2 million members. It works to defeat school-choice proposals through lobbying and litigation.

People for the American Way, 2000 M St., N.W., #400, Washington, D.C. 20036; (202) 467-4999; www.pfaw.org. This grass-roots organization promotes First Amendment rights through public-education programs.

---

[2] Figures from the Children's Educational Opportunity Foundation of America (CEO America).

[3] The Center for Education Reform, "National Charter School Directory 1998-99."

[4] Sandra Feldman, "Let's Tell the Truth," *The New Republic*, Nov. 24, 1997.

[5] Quoted in "School Vouchers," *USA Today*, December 18, 1998.

[6] Gerald Tirozzi, "Vouchers: A Questionable Answer to an Unasked Question," *Education Week*, April 23, 1997.

[7] Quoted in Derrick Z. Jackson, "The Corruption of School Choice," *The Boston Globe*, Oct. 28, 1998.

[8] A recent survey by an African-American think tank showed black support for vouchers is declining, contradicting the findings of the 1998 Gallup Poll. The 1998 telephone survey by the Joint Center for Political and Economic Studies found that between 1997 and 1998 African-American support for vouchers declined from 57 percent to 48 percent. Results are posted on the center's Web site, www.jointctr.org/selpaper/poll_edu.htm.

[9] See *Facts on File*, 1998, p. 409.

[10] For a summary of related Supreme Court rulings, see David Masci, "School Choice Debate," *The CQ Researcher*, July 18, 1997, pp. 625-648.

[11] Quoted in Mark Walsh, " 'Green Light' for School Vouchers?" *Education Week*, Nov. 18, 1998.

[12] Howard P. Berkowitz, "Think Twice About Vouchers," on the ADL's Web site at

www.adl.org/frames/front_opinion.html. The ADL opposes tuition vouchers.

[13] Joe Loconte, "Will Vouchers Undermine the Mission of Religious Schools?" *Policy Review*, January-February 1999.

[14] "Barriers, Benefits and Cost of Using Private Schools to Alleviate Overcrowding in Public Schools," Final Report, U.S. Department of Education, Office of the Under Secretary, 1998.

[15] Quoted in Laconte, *op. cit.*

[16] For background, see Charles S. Clark, "Attack on Public Schools," *The CQ Researcher*, July 26, 1996, pp. 649-672.

[17] Milton Friedman, "The Role of Government in Education," in Robert A. Solo (ed.), *Economics and the Public Interest* (1955), pp. 127-134.

[18] Quoted in Clark, *op. cit.*, p. 662.

[19] John E. Chubb and Terry M. Moe, *Politics, Markets and America's Schools*, 1990.

[20] Figures are from the Wisconsin Department of Public Instruction.

[21] Press release, Feb. 2, 1999.

[22] Versaci's comments were made in a press statement the day of the House vote.

[23] See Mark Oswald, "Government shutdown looming if haggling persists," *The Santa Fe New Mexican*, March 23, 1999.

[24] Jay P. Greene and Nicole Mellow, "Integration Where it Counts," a paper prepared for delivery at the 1998 Annual Meeting of the American Political Science Association.

[25] For background, see Charles S. Clark, "Home Schooling," *The CQ Researcher*, Sept. 9, 1994, pp. 769-792.

Bibliography

Selected Sources Used

Books

Hanus, Jerome J. and Peter W. Cookson, Jr., *Choosing Schools: Vouchers and American Education*, American University Press, 1996.

Two university professors with opposing views on school vouchers debate the issues of whether vouchers will force public schools to improve, whether vouchers are constitutional and whether vouchers will improve student achievement.

McGroarty, Daniel, *Break These Chains: The Battle for School Choice*, Prima Publishing, 1996.

A fellow at the Institute for Contemporary Studies gives a blow-by-blow account of how low-income parents in Milwaukee fought to establish the nation's first voucher program and keep it alive despite opposition from the educational establishment and voucher opponents.

Articles

Feldman, Sandra, "Let's Tell the Truth," *The New Republic*, Nov. 24, 1997.

The president of the American Federation of Teachers argues that the momentum for vouchers will dissipate once the public understands the long-term impact. Vouchers will mean giving up on American public education, siphoning off as much of its funding as possible to enable a few "deserving poor" to go to private — mostly religious — schools, she argues.

Loconte, Joe, "Will Vouchers Undermine the Mission of Religious Schools?" *Policy Review*, January-February, 1999.

Voucher programs could end up being the Trojan Horse that exposed religious education to greater government control, argues Joe Loconte, William E. Simon Fellow in Religion and a Free Society at the conservative Heritage Foundation. As a result, many private schools will opt out of such programs and the choice movement could be dead on arrival, he contends.

Peterson, Paul E., "Vouchers and Test Scores," *Policy Review*, January-February 1999.

In preliminary results, this Harvard professor finds that students in the fourth and fifth grades in a private voucher program in New York City improved more in reading and math than their cohorts who were not chosen for the program. However, for students overall, in grades two through five, the difference was only 2 percent in both subjects.

Walsh, Mark, "'Green Light' for School Vouchers?"

Education Week, Nov. 18, 1998.

The author discusses the impact of last November's U.S. Supreme Court decision not to review the Wisconsin ruling that school vouchers for parochial students are constitutional. Even though the court did not comment on the ruling, the court's inaction opened the way for voucher advocates to push for more state voucher programs.

Reports

"Barriers, Benefits and Cost of Using Private Schools to Alleviate Overcrowding in Public Schools," Final Report, U. S. Department of Education, Office of the Under Secretary, 1998.

A recent Department of Education study found that 66 percent of urban sectarian schools surveyed probably would not join a voucher program that exempted students from religious activities, and 46 percent would probably balk at requirements that they select students randomly.

"Charter School Laws: State by State Ranking and Profiles," The Center for Education Reform, November 1998.

This report by a pro-charter school organization evaluates state charter school laws according to whether they are weak or strong, and examines how they work in practice when implemented by local and state officials.

"Just Doing It: 1998 Annual Survey of the Private Voucher Movement in America," Children's Educational Opportunity Foundation of America.

This report summarizes how the private voucher movement grew from a single program in Indianapolis in 1991 to 34 programs serving 12,684 students in the 1997-98 school year.

Rees, Nina Shokraii and Sarah E. Youssef, "School Choice: What's Happening in the States," The Heritage Foundation, 1999.

The report gives an exhaustive state-by-state rundown of existing and proposed school-choice programs and related news.

Witte, John F., "Achievement Effects of the Milwaukee Voucher Program," Department of Political Science, Robert La Follette Institute, University of Wisconsin-Madison, Feb. 7, 1997.

A University of Wisconsin political science professor finds that voucher students showed only negligible test-score gains compared with non-voucher students even though they benefited from factors that usually increase educational achievement, such as parents' education, socio-economic status and parents' academic expectations.

White House Asks Court for Voucher Ruling

By Linda Greenhouse

In the first sign that a new legal team is shaping the government's advocacy before the Supreme Court, the Bush administration is asking the justices to uphold an Ohio program that offers Cleveland parents tuition assistance to send their children to private schools, including religious schools.

Of the 3,700 children enrolled in the program, 96 percent attended religious schools. The United States Court of Appeals for the Sixth Circuit, in Cincinnati, ruled late last year that Ohio's Pilot Project Scholarship Program "clearly has the impermissible effect of promoting sectarian schools" and was therefore unconstitutional. Ohio asked the Supreme Court to hear the case, and the justices will consider that request when they return from the summer recess.

In a brief filed late last month in support of Ohio's petition, Theodore B. Olson, who was confirmed as the solicitor general in May, said that it was "in the nation's interest" for the court to take up the case.

Mr. Olson said policy makers needed to "know, without further delay, whether such programs are a constitutionally permissible option for expanding education opportunity for children enrolled in failing public schools across America, or whether other solutions must be sought for this critical national problem."

The brief said the appeals court's ruling, which was based principally on a 1973 Supreme Court decision that struck down a tuition reimbursement program in New York, was "at odds with" and "out of step with" the Supreme Court's more recent interpretations of the First Amendment's Establishment Clause. Policies that "benefit religion only indirectly as a result of the private choices of the program's beneficiaries" are constitutional, Mr. Olson said.

In a case like this, it is unusual for the solicitor general's office to file a Supreme Court brief until the justices agree to hear the case or ask for the solicitor general's view on whether they should hear it. Filing a brief at this early stage is a way for the administration to put its position on the record and to send a signal to the court of the high priority the administration attaches to the issue.

In the last few years, several cases have reached the court involving various approaches to assisting parents with private school tuition, any one of which might have provided a reason for the justices to address the question of "school choice," as proponents of the voucher program usually refer to it.

The Clinton administration did not file briefs in any of the cases, and the court did not accept any of them. In 1998, the justices permitted a voucher program in Milwaukee to remain in effect without reviewing the Wisconsin Supreme Court decision that had upheld it.

During the presidential campaign and the early months of his administration, President Bush was a strong supporter of vouchers. Democrats in the House of Representatives and the Senate stripped a voucher provision from Mr. Bush's education bill this year.

The Cleveland voucher case has been seen for several years as a likely Supreme Court test of the concept's constitutionality, and the justices were clearly aware of the case well before receiving Mr. Olson's brief. In November 1999, the court voted, 5 to 4, to grant a stay that permitted the Cleveland program to continue after a judge in Federal District Court had issued a preliminary injunction and before the United States Court of Appeals for the Sixth Circuit had a chance to take the case. Granting a stay of a lower court's decision is usually a strong indication of the justices' interest in eventually hearing the case.

Index